Praise for *The New Millionaire's Playbook*

"*Gordy Bal walks the walk and invites others on the path with him. This stuff is life-changing.*"

— **Dave Asprey**, founder of Upgrade Labs and four-time *New York Times* best-selling author

"*Gordy Bal is a revolutionary thinker who doesn't tell you what to think, but how to think. His message of raising human consciousness is deeply important for this time.*"

— **Dr. Shefali**, conscious parenting expert and *New York Times* best-selling author of *The Conscious Parent* and *The Awakened Family*

"*Gordy Bal is one of those unique humans who can get to the core of who you are in just minutes through humour, honest questions, and deep insights.*"

— **Dr. Gabor Maté**, best-selling author of *When the Body Says No* and *In the Realm of Hungry Ghosts*

THE
NEW
MILLIONAIRE'S
PLAYBOOK

THE NEW MILLIONAIRE'S PLAYBOOK

7 KEYS TO UNLOCK FREEDOM, PURPOSE, AND ABUNDANCE

GORDY BAL

HAY HOUSE, INC.
Carlsbad, California • New York City
London • Sydney • New Delhi

Published in the United States by: Hay House, Inc.: www.hayhouse
.com® • *Published in Australia by:* Hay House Australia Pty. Ltd.: www
.hayhouse.com.au • *Published in the United Kingdom by:* Hay House
UK, Ltd.: www.hayhouse.co.uk • *Published in India by:* Hay House
Publishers India: www.hayhouse.co.in

Cover design: The Book Designers
Interior design: Joe Bernier
Interior photos/illustrations: Tammy Pham

**Cataloging-in-Publication Data is
on file at the Library of Congress**

Hardcover ISBN: 978-1-4019-7629-3
E-book ISBN: 978-1-4019-7630-9
Audiobook ISBN: 978-1-4019-7631-6

10 9 8 7 6 5 4 3 2 1
1st edition, August 2023

Printed and bound by CPI Group (UK) Ltd, Croydon, CR0 4YY

*This book is dedicated to my three sons,
Jaxon, Jovie, and Julian. May your spirits
soar high and your lives be filled with joy and
magic. I love you through and through.*

**To get the full experience
of this book, go to:**

newmillionairesplaybook.com

**You'll find downloads and
resources to support your
journey toward freedom,
purpose, and abundance.**

CONTENTS

INTRODUCTION

VISION OF THE NEW MILLIONAIRE

We cannot solve our problems with the same thinking we used when we created them.

— **ALBERT EINSTEIN**

Right now, you are better positioned than at any other time in history to design the life of your dreams—a life and reality where everything is possible and you are able to manifest whatever it is you wish. The abundant access we have to exponential technologies as well as the revitalization of ancient wisdom give us godlike superpowers that have been hidden from us for far too long. We have everything we need to live a mind-expanding, heart-opening, and soul-nourishing existence.

So, why does it seem at times like the world is on the brink of falling apart? At this precise moment, you are reading these words right here, right now, because there is much about the way the world works that isn't sitting right with you. You know on some level deep inside of you that the game is rigged, and you are ready to see behind the veil.

You are a part of a growing group of humans that are waking up and not only questioning the systems we live within but also questioning reality itself. You find yourself asking things like: *How does the world actually work? What is the nature of our reality, and what is the meaning of life? What is my purpose?* I, too, have been exploring these questions over the last 20 years and am certain that we are connected and meant to be here and now. I'm grateful and excited to be connected with you at this unique time in history, where we have the power to change the trajectory of the future and live in alignment with our truest selves.

Together, we'll go on a journey where I'll show you that your dream life is closer than you may think. Whether you are looking to upgrade your relationships, purpose, finances, location, lifestyle, or simply your understanding of the way the world operates, you will have the opportunity to release the shackles that bind you and become free.

I played the Old Millionaire game for far too long. I was a walking cliché of a person who thought money could buy happiness, and all I had to show for it was a big bank balance and a bankrupt soul. I had a yearning for meaning, purpose, and joy. You may be in a similar place right now. I was fortunate that I had the resources to embark on a decade-long journey to explore consciousness. In some ways, I didn't have a choice, since despite business and material success, there were days I couldn't drag myself out of bed.

I was experiencing extreme bouts of what scientists call *cognitive dissonance*—internal distress from feeling like my actions and beliefs were misaligned. It was as though I had climbed the summit of a mountain and there was nothing but emptiness at the top. I had to face myself as I realized my life was a façade and that I had bought into a fraudulent dream. I could blame societal programming—and, believe me, for years, I did—or I could share with you how I deconstructed that programming and learned to think my own thoughts.

Think your own thoughts.

Yes, this is critical and doable. In short order, you will see what it means to think your own thoughts. All that noise—from old programming, media, parents, societal expectations—gets muted and replaced by your own thoughts. You will begin to see your thoughts as the most powerful currency you have and learn how to invest them to create *your* reality, on *your* terms. The universe does indeed conspire for us and through us, and I will show you how you can interface with it to shapeshift your experience. Your *mental wealth* will grow and be your foundation for becoming the New Millionaire.

In my consciousness journey, I went all in. I spared no expense in terms of time, money, or soul to figure out what I was meant to do on planet Earth and how I could turn my frustration and hopelessness into love and joy. I spent over a million dollars traveling, studying, and experimenting. The best part, and what I can't wait to tell you more about, is that I discovered a small group of people who had *cracked the code* on living an amazing life. Instead of being used by technology, they are using it. They live to thrive rather than survive. Their work, which is connected to their purpose, creates *freedom, purpose,* and *abundance.*

As my kids would say, *they're crushing it, dude*. And now, because these people let me into their world as a friend and business associate, they have helped me unlock the formula so *you can do this too*.

Clarity of purpose is a hallmark of New Millionaires. You will also see that earning money goes hand in hand with consciousness and that you can create abundance while living your purpose. From that place, alignment and resonance begin to show up. Once you gain the power to think your thoughts, you stop playing a rigged game. Since your dream is linked to your humanity, you will cherish your capability to effect positive change on *any* scale.

As you gain clarity in what you are meant to do, your conviction grows. Whether it's raising capital, recruiting talent, or acquiring customers, your shift of mindset will become contagious and be your strongest source of influence. This book provides a process to clarify your purpose through seven Keys. Armed with this, you have a good chance of being led to epiphanies where the intersection of commerce and consciousness create abundance. As you see how simple the seven Keys are to apply, you'll feel a new sense of hope. The Keys are:

1. Unplug from the Matrix

2. Discover Your Purpose

3. Measure Your MEPS

4. Find Your Mission to MARS

5. Build Resilience, Resources, and Relationships

6. The Wealthy Spiritual Warrior

7. MAGIC: The Secret Pathway to Unlock Unlimited Possibilities

Let's now zoom in on the term *New Millionaire* and give it a proper definition.

DEFINING *NEW MILLIONAIRE*

What do you think of when you hear the word *millionaire?* It might bring to mind images of the old definition of millionaire—someone who chases money, uses relationships as a form of currency, and focuses on profit over purpose. This lifestyle leads to feeling trapped and constricted and leaves little time for nourishment and rest. This way of being is part of the old paradigm. The new millionaire operates on a different level. Money chases them. They experience freedom, purpose, and abundance. They have fulfilling relationships and they balance their mental, emotional, physical, and spiritual well-being with intention. They generate more profit through living their purpose.

The new millionaire's measurement of success is impact, not money. You positively impact one million lives, starting with your own. Health is wealth, and financial abundance flows as you live your purpose. With new awareness and tools, you begin to play the most magnificent game you can and enjoy the glorious experience of being alive on this amazing planet at this precise moment in human history. Your time is your own, your relationships are harmonious, and you feel a sense of peace. You are moving mountains with little or no effort.

We need resources, and that requires money. This is not a book about how to live off the grid. It is a book, however, that isn't afraid to tell you how fragile the grid and legacy systems are. But, rather than be fearful, we'll focus on building resiliency, creating abundance, and unplugging from toxic societal norms to the extent that you can. A part of that means earning money to solidify yourself financially.

Imagine this:

- You are connected to your purpose. The work you are doing is positively impacting the lives of others. If it doesn't already, you see how it will impact millions.

- You have a healthy relationship with your phone and seamlessly use technology to make your life better.

- You feel confident that you have full sovereignty over your funds and feel excited about the projects you are invested in.

- You feel connected to the people in your life and cultivate easeful relationships in a fun and joyful way.

- You look in the mirror and feel love toward the reflection looking back.

Welcome to your new reality. It only gets better from here.

THE GREAT WEALTH TRANSFER

We are living at an unprecedented moment in history, when an astronomical amount of money will be changing hands. Instead of designing Old Millionaire mousetraps to *extract* that money, with your shift in consciousness, you'll be able to *magnetize* that money. As a result, *money will chase you.*

As Gen Z and millennials inherit mass wealth from baby boomers, we're looking at a "Greater Transfer" of wealth than we've ever seen. *Forbes* reported that in America alone, more than $68 trillion will be inherited by millennials from baby-boomer parents before 2030. To put this into context, if you were to stack a trillion dollars in one-hundred-dollar bills, it would be twice as high as the International Space Station—that's 635 miles above Earth's crust.

This wealth transfer is happening at a time when we are experiencing a new generation of humanity that is more focused on building a regenerative economy. It's incumbent on us to lead the way. You could say I'm overly optimistic or accuse me of attempting to speak this into existence, but I do believe that the next generation cares more about the collective well-being than generations before. I see a shift in values where instead of hoarding and controlling, there's a real desire to connect more deeply with others and with nature.

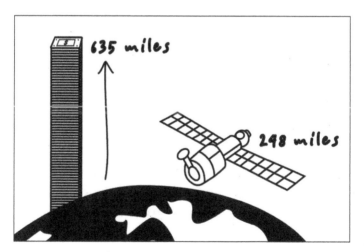

As an investor, I see that the companies getting funding are ones that care about consciousness. That's how you *magnetize*. You show up authentically with a desire to serve and connect, and opportunities (and money) will find you. Part of our journey together will be to create the frequency that attracts what you are seeking.

We're not buying into the "suffer now to climb the corporate ladder" mentality that created massive wealth for corporations as wages stagnated. The Great Resignation, Quiet Quitting, and WallStreetBets are all indicative of a change in consciousness. As the wealth disparity grows and social media propagates envy, more and more people are refusing to be cogs in the corporate wheel. The days of sacrificing our mental health for a company, especially one without a soul, are over. There is a better way.

Becoming a New Millionaire means *more choices*. Some 18-year-olds, instead of going into debt for a university degree, know where to find opportunities that allow them to do good for themselves and for the world. I know people in their 20s and in their 70s choosing to be digital nomads who live and play all over the world. Those who are most awake have found the balance of being connected to the world (via technology) and connected to themselves (via self-exploration and nature).

Entrepreneurs and CEOs have the opportunity to serve by taking on a bigger mentor role, lifting others up, and injecting conscious principles into all of their decisions and negotiations. Having more sovereignty gets you out of the rat race and into more purposeful work. Instead of chasing something that you can never attain by looking externally, you realize that everything you need is internal.

We are coming into an awakening that has the potential to challenge the current capitalist paradigm—one that is not only causing extreme social damage to mass groups of people, but environmental damage that could lead to our own extinction. Before we get to that dire point, we have the power to take responsibility for our capital and to coexist not only with all of humanity, but also with all other life forms (including our future AI overlords . . . only half kidding).

We are emerging into a new type of consciousness where we are deeply connected with nature, coexisting with exponential technology, and leading from a place of love—where we see ourselves as an integral part of the universe. This state of humanity takes us to a place where we see our investments as in direct correlation with our state of consciousness in the moment. Our thoughts are made manifest through the way we spend our dollars. We have the power to tap into our greater wisdom and change the energetic value of money.

We must move from **ME** consciousness to **WE** consciousness, which is why we need a Conscious Thought Revolution.

CONSCIOUS THOUGHT REVOLUTION

We are on a profound inner journey to becoming New Millionaires. A Conscious Thought Revolution is our gateway. The seven Keys that I will share with you unlock the portals of the practical steps for moving through that process.

We're going to spend a lot of time exploring where thoughts come from and how we can take back the power to *think our own thoughts*. In fact, the first step to embarking on a Conscious Thought Revolution is divorcing yourself from the voice that tells you that you are not enough. This requires shifting from *thoughtlessness* to *thoughtfulness*. From here, you can create your own beliefs—beliefs not held as a rigid system, but instead with a constant curiosity about yourself and the world you want to live in.

What is a Conscious Thought Revolution?

Let's break it down.

CONSCIOUS

To be aware and responsive to one's surroundings. In other words, to be awake.

THOUGHT

An idea or opinion formed by our mind. It is not reality itself, yet it does *create* our reality.

REVOLUTION

An overthrow of a certain social order to bring forth a new system. It is a complete change in the fundamental institutions of society.

Piecing these definitions together, **Conscious Thought Revolution** is a mission to wake up, become aware of how our thoughts create our reality, and break through outdated paradigms to pave a new way forward.

MY OWN CONSCIOUS THOUGHT REVOLUTION

As a child of the Internet age, by the time I was 15, I dove deep into the world of Internet marketing and soon learned how to mine attention. There's a system to it, and I learned to hack it. A few keystrokes here and a few more there, and I succeeded in getting inside people's heads to stimulate their desires. Even without artificial intelligence or the complex algorithms that exist today, I saw that those who knew how to mine attention were beginning to take over our thoughts.

As I observed the inner workings of their operations, I learned quickly how to use the language of fear, greed, and urgency to persuade people to click through to a website and take out their credit cards. I learned that simply changing the color of a button from blue to orange could double the number of conversions because of the way humans psychologically react to different colors. Yes, it really was that easy. Across the marketing and media industries, there was an arms race for more tech, more tools, and more power to take over people's minds. The money was ridiculous. It also put me on a win-lose course. My wins were at the expense of those whose attention had been mined.

By 20, I was running multiple businesses while studying psychology at the University of British Columbia. This allowed me to combine marketing, psychology, and technology to make even more money. Before long, I was running a call center business (boiler-room style), a government student loan business, a mutual fund business, an online casino affiliate business, and an ad arbitrage business. In a world full of acronyms, the one that dominated my thoughts was *CTR*: click-through rate. In online advertising, CTR is the key metric that determines success.

The click-through rate is the ratio of users who click on a specific link to the number of total users who view a page, e-mail, or advertisement. Your skill at growing CTR is determined by how well you convert eyeballs to clicks. I was winning the money game I thought I was supposed to, yet I was finding myself depressed, unhealthy, and numb.

Then 9/11 happened. This was the first time I really tuned in to a global event that changed the world as we knew it. I did plenty of soul-searching and started to connect the dots that were invisible to the naked eye. It would have been great to have friends and family who weren't afraid to challenge the traditional narrative and who could unpack what was going on. When I say we should "question the narrative," I mean *all* narratives. I had unanswered questions about 9/11, just as I had questions about what it meant to "make a living" and about how the world actually works.

As I continued my exploration, which included plenty of finger-pointing, it wasn't long before my fingers pointed in an uncomfortable direction: right back at me. Suddenly, hard questions were being launched my way as I asked, *Why do I choose fear over love? Why is money my scoreboard for success? And what is the endgame? If the game to accumulate as much money and power as possible is rigged, then what?* When I couldn't answer that last question, I hit a wall. Instead of continuing to look outward, I needed to look inside.

This inward journey brought on a familiar sense of discomfort that I was finally ready to sit with. Instead of numbing myself not to feel it, I became present to all the things inside me that I was not facing. This self-reflection revealed that I was as guilty as anyone for putting financial gains above community and personal well-being.

In 2007, upon waking up and seeing a record six-figure day, I acquired the domain name CTR.com for even more than that. I thought I was clever and would build a technology platform that helped advertisers increase their click-through rate. While the mainstream press was celebrating how much more efficient technology had made us, no one spoke about the losers (that is, most of the people using technology).

There was also a win-lose battle happening in my life. The more my wallet won, the more my soul lost. This fell in lockstep with Big Tech and Big Finance: profits rose at a steep pace, right alongside obesity, depression, anxiety, and environmental destruction. The money was too easy for everyone. And the boom led to a bust. In 2008, the global financial crisis destroyed wealth for a lot of people. I realized that few were asking the same questions I was, such as, "Why are the 'too big to fail' banks who created the crisis not being penalized?"

As disgusted as I was by the bailouts, it taught me that being angry and staying in victim mode prevented me from seeing opportunities. As legacy financial systems were teetering on the verge of collapse, Satoshi Nakamoto's white paper on Bitcoin was published. Suddenly a new money system was proposed that would give power back to the people. It would be decentralized (meaning no government control), and currency could be programmed with a new set of rules and principles that the community at large could agree on and co-design. A new game could be designed and played by all. To me, it was a nine-page tapestry of hope interwoven with smart technology.

Gradually I realized that consciousness was the only way to rectify the game. I went deeper to explore the link between brain development and human potential. I began to redefine capital beyond traditional means and to view thoughts as investments. And as we shift our thoughts, so we deploy our capital.

And as we shift our thoughts, so we deploy our capital.

As I started to express my truth—that consciousness is my path—I found my way to the right people and the right events. In 2015, in a deep state of vision questing, I realized that our planet does not need a higher click-through rate. What it needs is a different kind of CTR: a Conscious Thought Revolution.

Two years later, I attended a transformative event with my dear friend Andrew to set goals for the year. Andrew was already living the life of the New Millionaire. He was building his first of three unicorns (billion-dollar companies) in blockchain and continuously upgrading his own consciousness while living deeply with a sense of purpose to create a much better world for all.

This was the moment when I finally said, "Enough is enough." Emerging from that workshop, I declared that I would use all my energy to create a Conscious Thought Revolution. My goal was clear: to measurably accelerate the evolution of consciousness. I knew what I had to do. Against the advice of everyone around me, I needed to shut down all business operations that were not dedicated to this mission and aligned with my soul. This meant I had to enter a place of uncertainty; I didn't know where money would come from and how I would pay my staff. I didn't even know how to tell my wife. Sukhi and I had three young boys at the time. Yet when I broke the news to her, she didn't panic or meet me with fear or concern. Instead, she looked at me with a deep sense of certainty and trust and said, "I don't care if we have to sacrifice for a while. I have your back."

It was that vote of confidence that gave me the courage to deliver the news to my business partner. His practical side has always been the perfect balance for my visionary side. I worried about his reaction, especially since my declaration meant turning off the faucet that was churning out massive revenue.

He got very serious with me. I braced for impact. He said, "You know that 'set and forget' plan for investing in crypto that we started a few years ago?" I wasn't sure where he was going with this, so I let him continue. "I just checked our balance, and it gives us four years of runway. I'm on the same page, brother. Not only do I want to devote all our effort to a Conscious Thought Revolution, but we have the capital and team to make it work."

"Oh! Plus," I added, "we already have that prime three-letter URL!" Buying CTR.com had been a prescient investment after all.

It happened: the stars aligned. This was evidence of how the universe conspires with us to manifest our own reality when we connect to our true purpose.

YOUR NEW REALITY

That was my story. Now it's time to write yours. Your goal is to uncover the truth of what it means to be wealthy, and to unlock freedom, purpose, and abundance. These ideas come together to show you a new way of living and a powerful path forward. This playbook provides all three and will lead you on a path to:

1. **Freedom.** The power to think, act, and live freely in accordance with your beliefs

2. **Purpose.** Your core "reason for being"; where life has clear meaning and direction, guided by an inner compass and deep knowing of who you truly are

3. **Abundance.** A state where all of your needs are met and there is no feeling of lack or scarcity; the experience of fulfillment that occurs beyond the material realm

The flow of the book has been carefully designed. The foundational work will lead you to an exploration that culminates in a Conscious Thought Revolution. At the end of every chapter, there are four to six "power plays" that lead you on a clear path to becoming a New Millionaire.

You have everything inside you to tap into your unique purpose and unapologetically live your life with freedom, purpose, and abundance. What you're reading will simply affirm that and give you a gentle, loving nudge to claim your life and become a New Millionaire.

Treat this as an opportunity to reconnect to the sacred that forever exists within you, and to the knowledge that is innately yours. It requires you to look deep within yourself, as well as all around you, and decide what is true and important to you. While I can lead you to the door, only you can use the seven Keys I give you to open it. I know how challenging it is to pave a new way, and I also know that it is so worth it. The life of your dreams is waiting on the other side.

Let's get to work creating a Conscious Thought Revolution.

Together . . . as New Millionaires.

UNPLUG FROM THE MATRIX: IT'S NOT YOUR FAULT

*Lift the veil that obscures the heart, and there
you will find what you are looking for.*

— **KABIR**

The Matrix was a cultural masterpiece that reflects the world we live in. The film depicts life as the elaborate deception of an evil cyber-intelligence. I've come up with another way to describe the real-world version of it. I see the Matrix as a simulated reality that is curated by an unconscious globally entrenched power network that uses its reach and influence to reinforce and retain its power and control at any cost, including the health of people and the planet.

The following might sound like it's coming straight out of a sci-fi movie. My intention is not to sow paranoia or feed into conspiracy theories. It might feel uncomfortable, but if you stay with me, you'll not only see hidden truths in plain sight, but you'll also see how you might have already experienced the Matrix in your own life.

A phenomenon known as *mass formation psychosis* occurs through the collective consciousness.[1] It is most clearly visible when a large part of a society places attention on a leader or a series of events, focusing it tightly on one small point or issue. Followers can be hypnotized and be led anywhere, even if it opposes their own wisdom and moral compass.

Being plugged into the Matrix makes one an NPC—a *non-player character*, in video-game-speak. An *NPC* is a term often used in video games, which has been adapted to describe individuals who seem to lack independent thought and behave like non-player characters. This term has been further linked to the Simulation Hypothesis, which proposes that our reality may be a computer-generated simulation. In this context, an NPC could refer to a person who appears to be programmed to repeat certain opinions or behaviors, akin to how a non-player character in a video game follows a predetermined script. In short, living according to the Matrix means we're letting someone else do the thinking for us.

The Matrix is a projected reality that is controlled and influenced by external inputs. The external inputs of technology, media, finance, family, organized religion, education, culture, food, and Big Pharma constantly activate our nervous systems, curate the reality we live in, and influence internal aspects of ourselves. This isn't the real reality. It's the "reality" that others want for us. These "others" have their own agendas, which likely differ from our own. We need to break free and create our own reality.

This system was externally created and is held up through systems of control. The documentary *The Social Dilemma* opened many of our eyes. The phrase "we are the product" circulated, and maybe a few of us started to see that Big Tech is winning at our expense. The documentary even explained how they did it, pointing at the problem without offering much in the way of solutions. Most of the people I know who watched the documentary said they were frightened for their kids. The more they learned, the more their fear increased.

It's no surprise that most tech entrepreneurs I know are vigilant about restricting screen time for their kids, just as Steve Jobs was and billionaire Mark Cuban and Reddit co-founder Alexis Ohanian continue to be. For those of you who haven't seen *The Social Dilemma*, get ready to have your mind blown. You will never look at social media the same way again, and you will understand even more why you must commit to unplugging from the Matrix.

There is a concentrated effort by these systems to curate our reality for us. We are being used as a source of fuel and energy for intentions that are not aligned with our highest selves or souls. We are also co-creating and perpetuating the Matrix by subscribing to these beliefs, systems, and frequencies that are influencing us.

START 'EM YOUNG

John F. Kennedy was on to something when he saw that our potential as humankind directly correlated with our education, and it was Nelson Mandela who wisely stated, "Education is the most powerful weapon you can use to change the world."

If education is what we need, why do we put our children in a system for more than a thousand hours per year that is failing them?

To truly understand how the education system has put us in the Matrix, we must go back to where it all began. Compared to the span of human biological history, schools are new institutions that go hand in hand with industrialization. As industry grew, support for public education grew, and what came next was a widespread, hierarchical educational system.

In 1902, John D. Rockefeller funded the General Education Board to provide major funding for the creation of the American public school system as we know it. Although it started as a private institution, due to his power and influence, Congress adopted the board in 1903. Most of the time, the truth is easily available for anyone willing to look. Rockefeller was far from subtle. He's on the record as saying, "I don't want a nation of thinkers; I want a nation of workers."

Industry wants worker bees who don't ask questions. Coal mines would run short of workers if their employees knew too much about the health risks. Assembly lines would fail if there weren't enough people to take orders.

Does that make Rockefeller "wrong"? Or does it simply show that he was acting out of self-interest? Perhaps he didn't have the benefit of understanding win-wins or the awareness to see that thinkers can also be productive workers. Nonetheless, an education system that keeps us plugged into the Matrix persists.

It seems like a no-brainer that schooling today should be different from what came out of the age of industrialization. But here we still are, and the common themes for education haven't changed—sitting at desks all day, bells herding students from one subject to the next, disconnection from the outside world, standardized testing defining students with letter grades, and classes divided by age.

There is a better way. This is why Sukhi and I started a nonprofit dedicated to funding new-paradigm education projects like the Xploration Centre. We created this vision around the future we see for our three sons. To succeed in a purpose-driven world, education must support the discovery of our children's unique superpowers so that they can co-create a new world—a world where they are measured by how they make a positive impact on humanity and the planet.

MANIPULATING THE BODY

It's not just the education system that contributes to this distorted reality. One of the reasons my friend Dave Asprey, author of *The Bulletproof Diet*, has connected with such a large audience is that he keeps reminding us how insidious the forces are that make us unhealthy. As he offers tools and guidance on becoming healthier, he helps us understand why we're frustrated and empathizes with our struggles. He also shows us how powerful the industrial food system is and how powerfully our own biology can work against us.

For example, additives in food have been scientifically formulated—designed by brilliant people using advanced technology—to achieve profits for Big Food by getting us hooked on its products. We're not bad or weak because we can't say no to the cookie. That cookie keeps getting harder and harder to resist because of outside forces (its ingredients, plus sinister marketing) and inside forces (our gut biome and undernourished cells).

It doesn't stop with food. When my six-year-old son said he wanted to watch a YouTube video that he'd seen with his friends, I was curious and obliging. After some digging, he found it and played it for me. The video was simply a set of hands unwrapping toys slowly. When I saw this, I got a serious case of the heebie-jeebies. My immediate reaction was confusion, followed by concern.

First, I'd never seen my child quite so captivated by anything, let alone someone just unwrapping a toy. Second, I could immediately tell there was a tactic being used to captivate such a young, susceptible mind. That's when I recalled hearing about autonomous sensory meridian response, known on the Internet as ASMR—which, I noted, just happened to appear in this YouTube channel's name. When I checked the channel's stats, I saw that it had more than 7.5 million subscribers and more than 3.5 billion views.

ASMR is an experience characterized by a tingling sensation on the skin that typically begins on the scalp and moves down the back of the neck and upper spine. In simpler terms, it's a pleasurable physical reaction caused by a sound stimulus. When searched on Google, top results included "Gentle Whispering ASMR," "ASMR Helping You Fall Asleep in Bed," and "ASMR Ear Massage and Brushing."

Although a fairly new Internet phenomenon, the actual cause-and-effect of ASMR is nothing new. In fact, Craig Richard, Ph.D., author of *Brain Tingles: The Secret to*

Triggering Autonomous Sensory Meridian Response for Improved Sleep, Stress Relief, and Head-to-Toe Euphoria, believes it is a genetic response that's designed to mitigate stress hormones and help us feel relaxed—so much so that ASMR has been called a "brain orgasm."

That made me curious—what happens when you continuously stimulate this neurological pleasure response unnaturally? In a survey led by Dr. Richard, 40 percent of 19,000 respondents reported that their experiences from watching ASMR videos had decreased or gone away over time.[2] The same way that pornography stimulates a response in the body that would naturally be promoted by sex, ASMR stimulates a physical response that would also be naturally promoted by an actual experience, such as being snuggled by a loved one.[3]

Why does this scare me? Because it shows how technology is making it more difficult to distinguish between real-life experiences and those fabricated to mine our attention. More importantly, we don't know the long-term impact on our well-being or our children's development.

We are moving toward a world where we have little to no control over technology and its effects on us. Not only is it being used to catch our attention, but it's also being used to alter our physical chemistry and the way we see the world. It speaks volumes that the people who seem to have the most fear and caution around the technology we use every day are the ones who are creating it.

IT'S NOT YOUR FAULT

It's not your fault that you're anxious. It's not your fault that you feel envy while scrolling Instagram. It's not your fault that you're worried that you won't have enough money. What you are seeing is *designed* to scare you. Most of us are losing at this game because it's rigged.

You're not to blame. It's not any of our faults that we are often trapped inside the Matrix. That gives me some comfort, as I hope it does for you as well. It also reminds us that we must take back our thoughts and reclaim our power.

Here are two things you can do:

1. Understand, at your core, that it's not your fault.

2. Know that as long as you see you have choices, you're not a victim.

Understanding that you have choices is a powerful perspective. It allows you to take back control. Recurring feelings of helplessness keep you in a rut, spinning your wheels with no hope of moving forward or having a breakthrough. We talked about how powerful the forces of attention-mining are. To thrive in the world of today, the key element is to take control of your own thoughts.

CREATE YOUR OWN REALITY DISTORTION FIELD

Once you unplug from the Matrix, you can create your own reality. To do this, you have to understand the concept of RDF, or *reality distortion field*. Our RDF is what we experience and co-create reality through. This is how we have the power to operate in alignment with the way we want to live our lives.

The Matrix and the reality distortion field go hand in hand. Think of the RDF as a movie theater screen onto which your reality is projected. For most humans, what is displayed on their screen is dictated by the Matrix. When you start to awaken, you realize that you can decide and determine what is displayed on that screen. What it looks like when we are living within the Matrix is very different from what it looks like when we are in control of our thoughts and choices.

Let's examine how we can use our consciousness to create the reality that we want by going deeper into the reality distortion field. It's been associated so closely with Steve Jobs that Techopedia's definition mentions him:

A reality distortion field (RDF) is a phenomenon in which an individual's intellectual abilities, persuasion skills, and persistence make other people believe in the possibility of achieving very difficult tasks. The term was coined by Apple employee Bud Tribble to describe former Apple Inc. co-founder, CEO, and chairman Steve Jobs's ability to encourage his team to complete virtually any assigned or delegated task.[4]

You know how powerful the mind is. Now imagine that instead of having your mind and thoughts used against you, you could harness that power to bring out the best in yourself and in others.

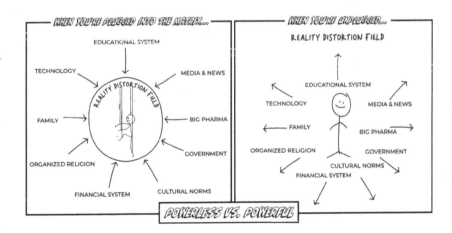

In a *Forbes* article, Adam Webb describes how, for Jobs, the RDF "worked like a personal force field; blocking out the fears, doubts, distractions, and negative thoughts that prevent most people from accomplishing their dreams. It also acted like a lens, reshaping Steve's perception of reality so that the impossible actually seemed probable."[5]

According to Webb, there are two simple steps to this process: (1) Accept that perception trumps circumstance, and (2) Use your thoughts to shape reality.[6] This is a fancy way of saying that once you think your own thoughts, you create your own reality. Creating your own RDF allows you to be an exceptional leader, offering others the gift of expanding their own boundaries.

When you think someone can do more than they think they can, you have the ability to infuse that thought into them and expand their reality. Steve Wozniak, the co-founder of Apple, describes what it's like to be on the receiving end of a leader's RDF. He said, "[Jobs's] reality distortion is when he has an illogical vision of the future, such as telling me that I could design the *Breakout* game in just a few days. You realize that it can't be true, but he somehow makes it true."[7]

UNPLUG FROM MEDIA

Talk to anyone in the media industry, and they will recite the mantra, "If it bleeds, it leads." No matter the form of media, its job is to hook our attention. We don't need to distinguish between traditional and social media, because the goal is the same: to scare us, keep us watching, and entice us to consume.

TV shows are called *programs*. The networks release their *programming* for each season. If we tune in, we are granting them permission to program our thoughts. Compared to what the Internet does to mine our attention, TV looks like child's play. Throw mobile into the mix and give the attention miners 24/7 access to our thoughts, and it's no wonder they have captured us.

The rise of 24/7 media, in all formats, has changed the way we live. It has allowed us greater access to people all over the world while disconnecting us from those right in front of us. Not only has it changed the world, but it has literally changed how our brains work.

Every time we are on social media, we are inundated with external noise. The average person spends two hours and 27 minutes on social media per day. Social media's ability to constantly capture and scatter our attention makes it harder to distinguish our own thoughts from the thoughts of others. We are literally giving away our mental energy to those who benefit from attention mining.

Through the concept of *variable-ratio reinforcement*, there is a constant stream of excitement and rewards in seeing new posts. Research has shown how this ability to capture attention has adverse effects on the brain, such as on attention capacities, memory, and social cognition.[8]

The more we use social media, the more difficult it is to ignore distraction in general. Not only does this affect our cognitive performance, but it shrinks parts of the brain associated with maintaining attention. Neuroplasticity, the ability of the brain to change, has a big effect on our attention and cognitive function.

Too many of us, myself included at times, are addicted to our screens. Every time we get a notification from an app, we are rewarded with a happy hormone release of dopamine. This rewires our brain to want more of it, leading to the cycle of social media addiction. If that's not enough, studies show that brain scans of heavy social media users look very similar to those addicted to substances or gambling.[9]

When you look at the data, it is clear that social media is taking more than it provides. On your phone, take a look at your daily average time spent on social media. You want this number to match the one *you set*. Choose what you think is a reasonable amount of time and stick to it, so you are not giving away your mental energy.

To help reclaim your attention, take a week-long social media detox. Delete all social media apps from your phone and commit to not looking at it for seven days. Notice how you feel throughout the week and where else you spend your time without the distraction of social media.

Does this sound frightening? If so, why?

Take the time to ask and answer these questions to get an accurate gauge of how addicted you may or may not be to your phone.

In the spirit of *adding* tools and not just taking them away, I'll tell you about something that did wonders for me: a sensory deprivation tank. I invite you to check out the research of John C. Lilly, who developed the tanks in the 1950s. Lilly was an American physician, neuroscientist, psychoanalyst, psychonaut, philosopher, writer, and inventor who shared ideas with Timothy Leary, Ram Dass, and Werner Erhard. Being in a flotation tank is one of the most effective ways to remove yourself from the Matrix, and it played a big part in my healing process.

I learned that when you are isolated from external stimuli, you are in a better position to explore the nature of human consciousness. In everyday life, up to 65 percent of your body's resources are being used to counter the force of gravity, and those are not active in a flotation tank. Because you're not experiencing sensory input, such as sound, smell, or touch, you can find space between your thoughts and yourself.

I did this weekly for a year, and it was instrumental in helping me heal my relationship with my father. It showed me, again, that once you alter your relationship to your thoughts, you will experience these types of miracles.

You have seen how external stimuli can take over your thoughts. If you don't do your part, they will forcibly influence your own internal aspects. You have also seen that the Matrix can be defeated.

As we wrap our arms around the Matrix, it helps to ask questions such as:

1. What's the motive of those who make the rules?

2. Who benefits from the situation?

3. Where is the money going?

4. Are the interests of the people making the rules aligned with your own?

Elon Musk said, "When I was a kid, I was wondering—kind of—what's the meaning of life? Like, why are we here? What's it all about? And I came to the conclusion that what really matters is trying to understand the right questions to ask. And, the more we can increase the scope and scale of human consciousness, the better we are able to ask these questions."[10]

Take it from Elon: try to understand what questions to ask.

For example, if someone labels you a conspiracy theorist, what question should you ask? Here are a few to try on:

1. Why am I being labeled for asking questions?

2. What is this person afraid of?

3. Where does their desire to make me wrong come from?

4. Does their opinion of me impact my opinion of me?

5. Who deemed being a "conspiracy theorist" a bad thing in the first place, and what was their objective?

Your ability to break free from the Matrix is directly related to your ability to ask good questions and see behind the generally accepted narrative. We must adopt a powerful mindset and be gentle with ourselves as we become more aware of our place within the Matrix. Because the external forces never stop, our work to connect to our own voice must be equally persistent. Reality is what you make of it. Let's leave the last word to Einstein, who said, "Reality is merely an illusion, albeit a persistent one"!

CHAPTER 1 POWER PLAYS

❑ Watch (or rewatch) *The Matrix*.

❑ Book a float session at a sensory deprivation tank.

❑ In your journal, write down five beliefs you have about the world. Then ask yourself:

1. Where did these beliefs come from?
2. Do I actually believe these things?
3. Do I have an emotional response if someone disagrees with these beliefs?

❑ Unplug from the media:

1. Check your daily screen time on your phone and notice where you spend most of it.
2. Take a weeklong social media and news detox. (Note: If you use social media for work, use these accounts solely from your tablet or laptop, or use a scheduling app to plan posts for the week ahead.)
3. After the week is done, reflect on what you noticed during your time without social media. Answer these questions:
   - Did your thoughts change?
   - What did you spend more time on?
   - What surprised you about the week off?
   - How do you want to readjust your relationship with social media?
4. Make changes around your long-term social media and news habits that support your chosen reality.

If you want to find out more about how to positively alter a child's relationship with technology, go to new millionairesplaybook.com.

2

DISCOVER YOUR PURPOSE

The meaning of life is to find your gift.
The purpose of life is to give it away.

— **PABLO PICASSO**

You are a unique being, brought to Earth to play out a unique purpose. In this chapter, you will examine your life and your purpose. You will look at the areas where you may have been misunderstood and judged for what you're not, rather than celebrated for who you are. It is here you will recognize your true gifts and unlock the true power you have within and allow it to enhance your life.

Rather than accepting who we innately are, too many of us conform to what others want us to be. This can lead us to become overachievers, constantly stressed and anxious, or perhaps too fearful to even try to reach our full potential.

Unfortunately, I speak from experience. Imagine waking up in a deep, dark depression, with the dread of an existential crisis, and not having enough energy to get out of bed. I learned the hard way what life looks like when you don't know your purpose.

I grew up in an emotionally tumultuous home. My earliest memories paint a picture of discord between my mother and father, and all I wanted as a kid was to fix it. My five-year-old mind fixated on money, and I believed that if we just had more money, everything would be okay. I told myself a story that if I made a lot of money, my parents wouldn't fight anymore and it would solve all of our problems. Because of all of the conflict at home, I got good at creating situations where everyone wins so that I could feel a sense of safety. Ironically, this is part of what led me to be good at business. At school, I created trading economies in a way that everyone got what they wanted. It was a survival mechanism—if I could just give everyone what they wanted, no one would be unhappy or angry.

I started making money at a young age, and it wasn't long before I had quite a lot of money. In my twenties, I had several online businesses that were generating a lot of revenue. The experience felt good, and I liked the fact that I seemed to figure out the money game far faster than my peers. But things at home didn't go the way I thought they would. They didn't get better—they got far worse. I had made making money my purpose, but my life wasn't any better.

My work habits led to poor health, and I was sad and depressed most of the time. It was disappointing to realize that what I'd worked for didn't solve the problem. I kept playing that game until world events like 9/11 and the bank collapse of 2008 made me step back and think about what was going on. Those events made me start to question the reality that I thought I understood, and I went deep into researching and learning about how money works, how government works, and the role that war plays. I wanted to know how all of the systems worked, and what I found disappointed and angered me. My depression deepened, and I got angry with the people around me who didn't see the same things I saw.

I concluded that the world was bad and filled with bad people. It was a dark time . . . and then I met my wife, Sukhi.

At the time, I can admit that I was a bit of a shadowy character. Sukhi saw through that and saw the light in me from the very beginning. She helped me see that light for myself. I remember the moment she introduced me to the idea of "checking in" with myself. It was such a foreign idea to me at the time. *Like, wait, there's a self I can check into?!* That was a catalyst. I realized there was another player in this game, and that player was me.

Falling in love with her gave me something important to fight for. She was the first person in my life that I felt safe enough to open up to. Our first few dates were out in nature. For the first time, I felt connected to nature in a deep way, since I never spent time outside while growing up in suburban Vancouver.

Sukhi's entrance into my life brought these big shifts that made me ask questions like "Who am I?", "What am I here for?", and "What's my purpose?" I realized that if I wanted to see a shift in the world that I had labeled as bad, then I had to start shifting myself. I couldn't point the finger outward and expect change. Change was an inside job.

And, sadly, I found that I wasn't alone. Anxiety disorders affect more than 40 million adults in the United States.[1] Worldwide, 85 percent of people do not enjoy their careers.[2] While it's challenging to overcome conditioning, it is possible.

As adults, we identify more with our roles in life rather than with a purpose. Most of the roles falling under the category of "occupation" consist of what we have to do, rather than what we love doing.

We are emerging into a purpose-driven world. When we do what we love and make a difference in the world, we find true fulfillment. This is when the magic happens. When I moved from being an entrepreneur focused on making *the most capital* to an investor focused on making *the greatest impact*, I experienced a complete shift in consciousness. This gave me a new sense of purpose and awoke an internal passion that had been previously dormant. I experienced higher levels of joy and fulfillment than I ever had before.

I share my story to show that you can make a similar transformation. I have come to discover that finding our purpose is the awakening of choosing ourselves and our desires and moving in the direction of what we truly want. Joy, freedom, fulfillment, and connection are just side effects. The true result is finding peace within yourself. So, with that, take a deep breath and soften into this moment.

You being here is enough. You choosing yourself is enough.

You being here is enough.
You choosing yourself is enough.

I still have to consciously remind myself of those words every single day, but I can assure you that with time, believing them gets a whole lot easier.

Stay open to the process and, most important, have fun. This is a celebration of the messy, wild, creative human that you are.

Now that we understand the importance of purpose, we can move toward two goals:

1. Discovering our purpose
2. Living our purpose

In Buddhist and Hindu philosophies, the word for purpose is *dharma*. Think of it as your cosmic order or universal truth—your truest potential. The following five steps will get you there. Read through them all first; then choose the tools that resonate with you and make this an active process.

Step 1. Fall in love with your brain

Step 2. Make a list of everything you're curious about

Step 3. Find the intersections of your criosity

Step 4. Play

Step 5. Turn your Passions into Purpose

STEP 1: FALL IN LOVE WITH YOUR BRAIN

Before you unlock the power of your mind, it's important for you to understand some of the pieces that make you who you are.

When we see ourselves as incapable of doing a task, many of us will decide that we're victims of the way we think or the way our brains operate. That way of looking at it leads to a perceived fixed problem with no solution and no way to alleviate it. We think that because we can't do math or art now, we'll never be good at it.

Instead of succumbing to the victim mentality, we need to accept the way our minds function and learn how to work with it. If you understand how your uniquely gifted brain works, you'll see it as a superpower rather than a hindrance.

A couple of years ago, I was invited to go through a protocol that helped participants discover their purpose. We did several assessments, all of which helped map parts of the brain. I took a test called Emergenetics, which showed that I'm imaginative, intuitive, and visionary—and that I'm a very conceptual thinker. What's more, my brain is unimodal, meaning I can think very abstractly and play with some very conceptual topics with ease. Turns out, unimodal minds make up less than 5 percent of the world. That's an incredible asset, but if you ask me to organize or work with Excel spreadsheets for hours on end, it's not going to happen.

For a long time, I thought my brain didn't work the way I wanted it to. When I realized what my brain could do (and what I shouldn't force it to do), I fell in love with it. I used to think of myself as mentally weak, but I now realize I have a superpower.

The point here isn't to stress about whether you have a unimodal mind like me. What I hope for you is that you learn how your brain works and fall in love with it, exactly how it is.

There's been a ton of research in neuroscience that helps. Much of it is being used in profiling tests that allow you to discover more about yourself.

When you learn about your brain, you learn what you're good at. You also stop being hard on yourself for the things your brain is not good at. For me, that's organization, detail, structure, and scheduling. I use Emergenetics when hiring so I can build a team with complementary skills.

In his book *The 6 Types of Working Genius: A Better Way to Understand Your Gifts, Your Frustrations, and Your Team*, author Patrick Lencioni breaks down genius into six types: wonder, invention, discernment, galvanizing, enablement, and tenacity. Lencioni points out that we all have areas of working genius, competency, and frustration.

According to the test, my areas of genius are wonder and galvanizing, which means I'm at my best when I use these gifts. I'm also most frustrated when I have to play in the sphere of organization. I agree with Lencioni that when you understand what you like and what you are good at, it helps you fall in love with your brain.

To be honest, Lencioni's assessment didn't blow me away. But because I'm always looking to fall in love with my brain, when a friend recommended it, I took the test. Part of your exploration is choosing the tools that resonate with you in order to understand yourself better. I'm not *shoulding* on you about taking any particular test. I'm sharing with you the value of curiosity and inviting you to explore different tools.

One tool that did make a big impact on me is the Gene Keys—a grand synthesis of practical wisdom to help guide you to a deeper understanding of yourself and your true potential. Understanding your Gene Keys can help you put the pieces of the puzzle together around who you are and why you are here, allowing you to break free from past conditioning that's out of alignment with your soul. When you're ready, go to GeneKeys.com/free-profile and get your free Gene Keys profile.

Whether or not you choose to do Gene Keys, I invite you to answer these questions that I found useful after getting my profile:

1. How would you describe your unique gifts and abilities based on what you know about yourself?

2. Do you feel as though you are currently living in a way that allows your true self to shine through?

3. What is one action step you can take to align with your most authentic self?

Along with Gene Keys, in the Resources section, I've provided other assessments that may be useful, including the Enneagram, DISC assessment, and Human Design.

By falling in love with your brain, you will be better equipped to better leverage it—and to connect with your purpose.

STEP 2: MAKE A LIST OF EVERYTHING YOU ARE CURIOUS ABOUT

Curiosity, like *creativity*, can be a triggering word. Many people do not see themselves as creative because of misconceptions of what a "creative person" is. Regardless of what we have been taught, everyone has innate creativity. Each one of us has unique ways our soul wants to express itself and create in the world.

If you don't identify as creative, that's a symptom of losing your curiosity. Allow yourself to imagine and to daydream, and give yourself permission to become who you truly are. A good question to ask yourself is, *What are the things I constantly want to learn or read about but continue to put off because I have "work to do"?* When you allow yourself to be curious, walls slowly come down, and you will find yourself happier, more alive, and more carefree.

I used to live life from a place of "knowing," and my perspectives were not as flexible or explorative. This created rigidity and contraction in my nervous system. The nervous system is the internal calibration system I learned to check in with to feel beyond my thoughts. When I allowed myself to become curious, I actually noticed my experience of time slowing down. My nervous system felt more relaxed, while my mind felt expansive and my heart felt open. Curiosity is one way to connect to the heart.

Make a list of 25 things you are curious about, that you would love to spend a weekend reading or learning about. If 25 things feels daunting, then you *really* need to do this ASAP. If you ask my kids what they are curious about, they will name a hundred things. When did we lose our childlike wonder? The more specific you can make the list, the better. Instead of writing "the environment," write "how trees communicate with each other." They do, which is something I learned because of my curiosity.

In less than three minutes, I wrote down 25 things I'm curious about: neuroscience, space exploration, the way of the samurai, intentional community, alternative energy (solar, wind, Nicola Tesla), Web3, decentralized autonomous organizations (DAOs) and non-fungible tokens (NFTs), vibrational frequencies, producing (beats, entertainment), eco-luxury, magic, psychedelic therapy, new-paradigm education, biomimicry, metabolism, Natural language processing (NLP), color therapy, regenerative farming, unconditional love, stand-up comedy, generosity and altruism, conscious parenting, dreams, martial arts, the exploration of consciousness, and gravitational waves.

Once you've created your list, share it with 10 people in your life. Ask them to write their own lists and share them with you. Then watch the magic unfold as you are guided to opportunities that mesh with your curiosity.

STEP 3: FIND THE INTERSECTIONS OF YOUR CURIOSITY

Where curiosities overlap, patterns will emerge. When we have a blank canvas, or a block of clay, there are no boundaries or limits to what can be created. This is a metaphor for life. Every day is a new page on which to create something fresh and inspiring.

The following process can be used to find the intersections of your curiosity:

1. Share your list with 10 people.

2. Ask them to share their lists and see what happens.

3. From your list, create a Venn diagram to see if there are common themes where things overlap that you weren't aware of before. For example, your 25 curiosities may fit into three to five activities or topics that encompass all your curiosities.

PATTERN RECOGNITION

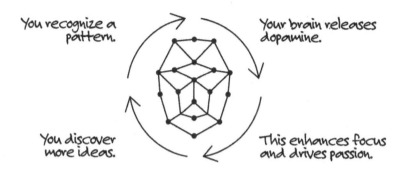

You recognize a pattern.

Your brain releases dopamine.

You discover more ideas.

This enhances focus and drives passion.

The act of simply asking people to write down their curiosities and share them sparks rich conversations and ideas that can be quickly put into motion. At a conference, I shared this exercise with a group that included the late Sean Stephenson. An inspiring speaker, Sean was also a board-certified therapist with a doctorate in clinical hypnosis. He took this exercise back to his practice and raved about its impact. Though it may sound obvious, I found it illuminating when Sean told me that curiosity is absent in depressed people. Apathy is the opposite of curiosity.

STEP 4: PLAY

As young children, it was a lot easier to be our most authentic selves. We were not yet programmed to fear what others thought of us or to act based on others' expectations. We were naturally drawn to play and did so just for the sake of joy, without worrying about how we would look, what we would get out of it, or whether there was a greater purpose to what we did.

There comes a point in each of our lives where the words of others penetrate us and cause us to separate from our souls. You probably heard someone—an adult, a childhood friend, a sibling, or a teacher—say something negative about what you loved as a child or about what you wanted to do when you grew up. That negativity or criticism probably caused you to step away from it one step at a time, until you forgot about it. As you grew up, the world around you slowly discouraged you from play, instead teaching you to focus on work. Every one of us has experienced this pattern, which has created generations of adults who are unhappy, uninspired, and unfulfilled.

If we look back at what we innately loved to do as children, we can receive clues about who we are meant to be in the world—in other words, our purpose. Play in the discovery process; it improves brain function and boosts creativity. I see play as a direct connection to purpose.

The world doesn't need more working adults; the world needs more humans who have come alive through living their true passions and purpose.

Use the following prompts to discover clues about your own purpose:

1. If there were no pressure, no rules, no "right" or "wrong," what would you create for creativity's sake?

2. When you were a child, what did you naturally love to do?

3. If you had one day to play, what would you do? Are you currently allowing yourself to do those things? What is stopping you?

The answers to these questions will help to unlock your purpose. Once you've reflected on them, it's time to bring play back into your life. Come up with one way you can incorporate what you discovered into your life *today* . . . and *every* day. At a minimum, commit to spending at least 10 minutes each day in a space of play, where you are following your passions and curiosities.

STEP 5: TURN YOUR PASSIONS INTO A PURPOSE

In this final step, make a list of 15 problems in the world you would like to see solved (or just list your desired solutions to them). Again, be specific. Instead of "climate change," you could write "renewable energy." The items you list will come from your life experience and the matters you find most important and relevant. Then, look at the intersections of your passions and the problems you listed. How can your passions be harnessed to help solve one of the problems?

I was able to come up with a list of problems in a few minutes: substance addictions, child abuse, world hunger, poverty, gender inequality, racial inequality, GMOs and declining soil health, outdated education systems, mass consumerism, deforestation, nonrenewable energy, sexual abuse, refugee crises, unconscious technology use, sugar addiction, the standard American diet, collapsing financial systems, corrupt governments, and the housing crisis.

See what comes up for you when you list the 15 massive problems that you want to see solved. What lights the fire inside you? What injustice do you seek to correct? What do you want to fight for? It's a bit cliché to ask, "What keeps you up at night?" but it's a solid question.

Imagine what would happen if instead of worrying about the world, you dedicated your life to impacting it.

However, it's one thing to know what you want to improve; it's another to have the skills to do so, and another still to know if you'd enjoy it. This brings us to ancient wisdom that has never been more relevant. It's what the Japanese refer to as *ikigai*—"a reason for being," also known as the Japanese secret to a long and happy life. When I looked it up on Wikipedia, I smiled when I read, "See also: *raison d'être, joie de vivre,* and meaning-making."

The impact of *ikigai* has been studied at length. According to research published by the National Institute of

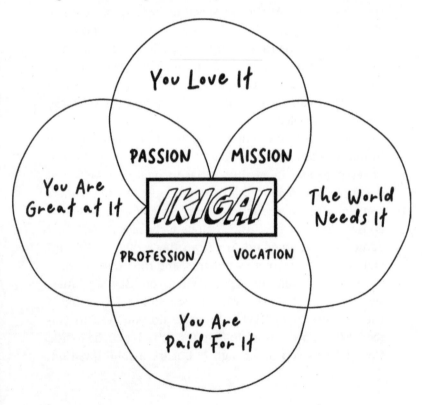

Health's National Center for Biotechnology Information, "*Ikigai* positively predicted well-being and negatively predicted depression . . . The findings support the importance for investigating *ikigai* in the West and the need for further exploration of *ikigai* as a potential means of bringing about benefit in mental well-being."[3]

The research also points to the health benefits, including reduced cardiovascular diseases. There you have it: finding your purpose is as serious as a heart attack. And there's the evidence that being a dad is a prerequisite for telling bad dad jokes. All kidding aside, we will explore the heart and its magic in more depth in Chapter 4.

Play with the suggested *ikigai* diagram and see if you can find your bullseye. In doing so, you can come up with a clear purpose statement that forever alters the lens through which you perceive reality.

PUT IT ALL TOGETHER TO CREATE YOUR STATEMENT OF PURPOSE

Now you've gone through five steps for finding your purpose. You understand yourself better and have fallen more in love with yourself. You've become more playful. Now you bring it all together to create your statement of purpose.

If I had a structural mind, my statement would have been something like this: "I help entrepreneurs discover their purpose."

Since I've embraced my brain map and found a way to be more playful, the following statement of purpose felt more authentic to me: "I awaken superheroes to unleash their magic within."

You have everything you need to create your statement of purpose. If you feel stress about identifying your purpose, reframe it as a signal to shift gears and move in a new direction. If you're not at peace, you're likely not living your purpose. Use your purpose as a way to filter opportunities. Your purpose can serve as the lens through which you look at business opportunities, relationships, etc. Also be aware that your statement of purpose can change. As humans, we are constantly growing and evolving; yet there are core elements of who we are that do not change. Let your statement be a road map that helps guide you where you are meant to be, starting with where you are today. Be okay with it changing along the way.

Suzy Batiz, founder and CEO of Poo-Pourri, is an example of someone who did the work to find what lights her up. She went bankrupt *twice*, which she attributed to being spiritually bankrupt. She said, "I searched my external world for that magic bullet that would magically catapult me out of some of life's lowest lows—sexual abuse, domestic violence, multiple bankruptcies. Eventually, I realized that I had the power deep within me. It was there all along; I just had to learn to look inside myself and to dig it out from under years and years of familial and societal programming."[4]

Batiz credits play and fun for her transformation. On her website, she wrote, "Once I learned to look within and harness the power of intuition, I transformed my life from a disaster to a dream come true and turned an ALIVE IDEA into a nine-figure empire."[5]

Pay attention to what happens *outside* your mind. Tuning in to what makes you feel alive creates resonance. I've been told by some of my more traditionally logical colleagues that this can be challenging, especially when we've been trained to ignore our emotions and be more head smart. If that sounds like you, this exercise is even more important.

I've outlined four ways for you to develop your resonance radar.

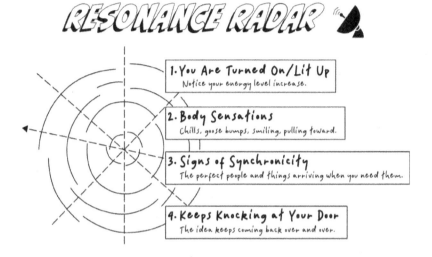

RESONANCE RADAR

1. **You Are Turned On/Lit Up**
Notice your energy level increase.

2. **Body Sensations**
Chills, goose bumps, smiling, pulling toward.

3. **Signs of Synchronicity**
The perfect people and things arriving when you need them.

4. **Keeps Knocking at Your Door**
The idea keeps coming back over and over.

Knowing your purpose creates opportunity. You attract those who want and need what you offer and repel those who don't resonate with your purpose. Instead of begging to do business with clients whom you may not even like, new clients will seek you out, asking you to give them your unique gift.

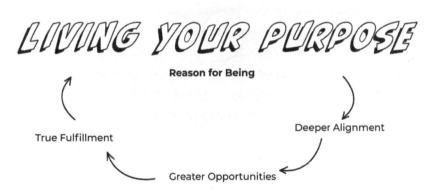

LIVING YOUR PURPOSE

Reason for Being

True Fulfillment

Deeper Alignment

Greater Opportunities

THE DANCER AND THE DANCED

When you're living your purpose, you're in a state of flow. Steven Kotler and Jamie Wheal broke ground on this topic, and I recommend their book, *Stealing Fire*. We'll examine the state where life happens *through* you later, in Chapter 7. It's a perfectly chaotic unfolding of the divine.

The cosmos is both chaotic and in perfect order. We are but tiny aspects of an infinite and expansive universe that is experiencing itself through each and every one of us. When we realize this beyond our intellectual minds, we can see that nothing actually matters, yet every "thing" is matter. We can surrender to a greater intelligence that underlies the fabric of the universe itself and enter a beautiful dance where we are both the dancer and the danced.

This can only happen in the present moment. It's not something you strive for. It's who you become.

For so long, the work I was doing was disconnected from who I wanted to be in the world. In discovering and articulating my own purpose, I changed the game, and I know you can do the same.

CHAPTER 2 POWER PLAYS

Use the following steps to discover your purpose:

1. Fall in love with your brain.

Choose two of the following tools to deepen your understanding of yourself and your brain.

- Emergenetics: https://emergenetics.com/
- Gene Keys: https://genekeys.com/free-profile/

- Enneagram: https://enneagramacademy.com/enneagram-test/
- DISC assessment
- Human Design

2. Make a list of everything you are curious about.

Make a list of 25 things you would want to spend a weekend reading or learning about.

3. Find the intersections of your curiosity.

From your list, create a Venn diagram to see where the items overlap to bring into focus a few common themes that you weren't privy to before. For example, the 25 curiosities may lead to three to five things that encompass all the curiosities.

4. Play.

Journal around the following prompts:
- If there were no pressure, no rules, and no "right" or "wrong," what would you create for creativity's sake?
- When you were a child, what did you naturally love to do?
- If you had one day to play, what would you do? Are you currently allowing yourself to do these things? What is stopping you?
- Commit to spending at least 10 minutes each day in a space of play, where you are following your passions and curiosities.

5. Turn your passions into a purpose.

- Make a list of 15 problems in the world you would like to see solved. Be specific.
- From your list, create a Venn diagram to see where items overlap to bring into focus any common themes that may have been hidden before (just as with the areas your 25 curiosities fell into). How can your passions be harnessed to help solve one of the problems?
- Use the template of the ikigai Venn diagram to clearly outline the different aspects of your purpose: what you love, what you're good at, what the world needs, and what you can be paid for.

6. Put it all together to create your statement of purpose.

- Come up with a statement that combines the items that you outlined above.
- Share the first draft of your purpose statement with three to five close people in your life and ask for their feedback using these questions:
    1. What parts really sound like you?
    2. What parts don't quite sound right?
    3. Is any part of the statement unclear?
    4. Does the statement encapsulate the energy and essence of the you that they know?

3

MEASURE YOUR MEPS

*You, yourself, as much as anybody in the entire
universe, deserve your love and affection.*

— THE BUDDHA

When we raise our own consciousness, we raise the collective consciousness. No matter the setting or source, I'm
constantly looking for tools that allow me to look within
myself to see the true essence of who I am as a human
being. In doing so, I can see that consciousness is the root
cause of all our issues. That's when I turn my attention
to raising my mental, emotional, physical, and spiritual
(MEPS) well-being.

By expanding our consciousness, we can begin to
evolve into the next iteration of humanity. There may be
no better example of how this works than the country of
Bhutan. In 1971, Bhutan stopped using gross domestic

product (GDP) as a measure of prosperity and instead shifted to gross domestic happiness (GDH). The country's approach targets the spiritual, physical, social, and environmental health of its citizens and natural environment.

Bhutan has thrived. According to the World Health Organization, between 1960 and 2014, life expectancy there more than doubled. Bhutan also enrolled almost 100 percent of its children in primary school and overhauled its infrastructure in the last 20 years.[1]

"It's easy to mine the land and fish the seas and get rich," said Thakur Singh Powdyel, Bhutan's minister of education. "Yet we believe you cannot have a prosperous nation in the long run that does not conserve its natural environment or take care of the well-being of its people, which is being borne out by what is happening to the outside world."[2]

The approach is spreading. As far back as 2013, the United Nations has embraced Bhutan's holistic approach to development, a move that was supported by 68 countries.[3]

We are seeing greater potential than ever as we shift our focus to raising our own consciousness. Let's all take a page from Bhutan and focus on our happiness. To do so, we start by measuring and improving our MEPS.

M is for *mental*, the computer between your ears. Having a sharp mental space sets the foundation for how you think, respond, and act, giving you the ability to be in control of your human experience. E is for *emotional*, or how you feel, your state of being. It colors how you view the world and your place in it, allowing you to feel safe and supported (first and foremost, by yourself). P is for *physical*, the vessel that holds your very essence. Supporting your physical body means existing in an optimal way through life. S is for *spiritual*, or the sense of your soul, your deeper self. Here resides the core of you, often forgotten, but deeply important to make the most of the human experience.

To become a New Millionaire, you want all four aspects operating at peak performance. And for all four elements, the key is to ask questions and explore more deeply the truth of who you are.

MENTAL WELL-BEING

The human brain is made up of more than a billion brain cells that each connect to more than seven thousand other brain cells. It's more complicated than a computer, and that alone is more than most of us can understand. It's safe to say, the brain is the most complicated object in the known universe.

We are an accumulation of our experiences—good and bad. Our brains are the hard drives that store all our memories.

While we may not even remember some of our experiences, they're still stored in our subconscious and are triggered every single day. Perhaps this is why we react to certain situations with insecurity or fear without realizing the connection to a past experience. It may be why we still feel insecure in our job or are afraid of commitment. Our subconscious goes back to our past and extends into the future we are creating. While we can't change our past, we can change our perception of it and how we respond to events in the present.

The mind is so complex, which is why I often say that we need to get *out* of our minds and *into* our hearts. Our thoughts aren't even real, yet they feel that way. Keep asking this question: Are you having your thoughts, or are your thoughts having you?

Thoughts are the most powerful currency. What does *currency* mean? Currency comes from the word *current*. An electric current is a stream of charged particles, such as electrons or ions, that moves through an electrical conductor or space. It is measured as the net rate of flow of electric charge through a surface or into a control volume. Similarly, your thoughts at the most fundamental level are electromagnetic reactions that occur in your brain and have a charge or value to them.

Think of your thoughts as the currency that you invest to create your reality. If you were to measure the value of your thoughts, how good are the investments you are making with them on a day-to-day basis toward creating your life and reality? Even though there isn't a Fitbit for thoughts, you must monitor them. Actually, in a way, we already do have a Fitbit for thoughts. That's what social media algorithms do—except they just use it for their benefit to make billions of dollars.

Big Tech is constantly monitoring our every click and scroll using complex algorithms to predict likes and desires. By tapping into our thoughts, it mines our attention to increase its profits. To reclaim power over our own minds, we must turn the tables on Big Tech.

Start by doing your own audit: measure the quality of your own thoughts.

Listen to the language of your inner dialogue—is it empowering or disempowering?

Check your phone to see the last 10 people you talked to, the last 10 people you texted, and the last 20 social media messages you read. Did they create fear and greed, or did you experience love and gratitude?

The best thing you can do is keep asking questions. Byron Katie, author of several best-selling books, including *A Mind at Home with Itself,* said, "To question what you believe is an amazing gift to give yourself, and you can have it all the days of your life. The answers are always inside you, just waiting to be heard."[4]

Katie has excellent tools on her website, TheWork.com, including four questions to ask any time a thought pops into your mind.

1. Is it true?

2. Can you absolutely know that it's true?

3. How do you react, what happens, when you believe that thought?

4. Who would you be without that thought?[5]

When you ask questions, you see that your thoughts aren't even real. They are simply thoughts. They can own you, or you can own them.

For better mental well-being, here are four questions to continue asking:

1. What are my thoughts saying right now?

2. Are they empowering or disempowering?

3. What would it look like to choose different thoughts?

4. Am I having my thoughts, or are my thoughts having me? What does that mean to me?

From here, we can go on and make choices that align with our highest mental well-being.

EMOTIONAL WELL-BEING

We can think about our emotional health like a computer's operating system that is meant to support our bodies in processing information. Every moment of the day, our body is processing multitudes of emotions as we experience them. If we can learn to be aware of the body's signals, we can engage with our emotions at a deeper level.

Most of us are unable to process our emotions in a healthy way. It is as though our storage is full, and we are unable to process anything without first clearing out old waste. When we experience different emotions that we don't want to feel and our operating system isn't able to process them, they go into a folder that keeps getting bigger and takes up all our operating system's capacity. Over time, our ability to function diminishes, and we barely have the bandwidth to deal with day-to-day tasks. Not only are we full of emotional backlog from childhood trauma and adverse events, but we also experience the emotional burden from politics, media, our friends and family, and many other external sources. Backlogged emotions are like a computer virus that slows down our operating system and makes us susceptible to information we don't want to receive.

The good news is that there is a way to clear our operating system. We have the ability to clear the emotional baggage that prevents us from living a free life. It starts with reconditioning what we were taught to believe about our emotions and truly understanding the importance of feeling our emotions as they come up. Instead of letting the hard drive fill up, we continuously clear it out and make space for what we truly want in our lives.

To do this, we need to face our emotions head-on and allow them to be felt and examined. We need to acknowledge the patterns of our emotions, which often stem from childhood trauma. Anger, sadness, shame, guilt, fear—none of these emotions are off the table. Instead of letting them fester and take up space, bring them to light and allow them to be experienced.

As we begin to clear the backlog, the bandwidth that was wasted on unproductive emotions is freed up. From here, we can begin to experience healthier relationships, calmer states of being, clearer thinking, and seeing the world through a lens that isn't obstructed by years of unprocessed emotions.

I recommend the following books that are extremely supportive in achieving emotional freedom:

- *The Body Keeps the Score* by Bessel van der Kolk
- *When the Body Says No* by Gabor Maté
- *Waking the Tiger* by Peter A. Levine and Ann Frederick
- *Listen* by Patty Wipfler and Tosha Schore

As we practice experiencing our emotions, we get better at receiving the signals before they manifest in our lives and bodies, allowing our system to function in an optimized state. For better emotional well-being, here are some questions to continue asking:

1. How can I assess my emotional awareness? And how can I raise it?

2. What am I truly feeling right now? Do I realize that my thoughts are influencing my feelings?

3. Am I feeling this feeling, or am I thinking this feeling?

4. What would I need to do to feel my feelings right now?

From here, we can go on and make choices that align with our highest emotional well-being. Once you master your emotions, your entire life will change. The lens through which you've been seeing the world will alter, and you'll learn that you have control over your environment and circumstances. That responsibility may feel scary now, but I assure you that it will set you on the path to freedom, purpose, and abundance.

I've found that some of my deepest emotional work takes place within my relationship with my wife. If we're committed to making our romantic relationships work, we have to search for the emotional residue of our upbringing and work to transform it. My relationship with Sukhi and my desire to be a better partner have led me to examine my own emotional conditioning. I realized that growing up, I lived in a household that didn't value women as equals, which impacted my marriage. Early on in our relationship, I still perpetuated gender roles and operated as though masculine was superior to feminine. Even though I knew on some level that this was not aligned with my deeper self, I did not know how to fix it.

Consciousness is not a linear path. Be wary of anyone who points to one teacher, book, or workshop and guarantees it will give you all the answers. That's why you have to keep searching. You never know when the right story or passage will make an impact. While studying the teachings of Guru Nanak, I came across this scripture:

> In a woman man is conceived, from a woman he is born, with a woman he is betrothed and married, with a woman he contracts friendship. Why denounce her, the one from whom even kings are born? From a woman a woman is born, none may exist without a woman.

This hit me like a ton of bricks. It led me to explore more deeply the divine feminine and the divine masculine, as well as the interplay between them. Men and women have both of these qualities; they transcend gender. I am still diving deep into this exploration. If you are in a romantic relationship with a partner, consider reading together *Intimate Communion*, by David Deida. This was a transformative process in my marriage.

As a husband and a father, I constantly ask what masculinity means. Books like *King, Warrior, Magician, Lover: Rediscovering the Archetypes of the Mature Masculine*, by Robert Moore and Douglas Gillette, have been helpful. They explain how the absence of initiation rituals has prevented boys from building confidence and self-sufficiency.

Initiation rituals vary by culture, but their purpose is the same: a rite of passage for a male to symbolically leave boyhood behind. The most extreme example was the Maasai lion hunt, where a boy was given a spear and a shield—and it was either kill or be killed. We often think of fraternities and the military as places for initiation rituals, and they expose both the positive aspects, like overcoming obstacles through shared challenges, as well as the negative aspects, like alcohol abuse and bullying.

Raising more conscious men in the world who understand the divinity in both the masculine and feminine will lead to a revolutionary shift in the liberation of women, who have been treated like second-class citizens for far too long.

As much as I have been studying masculinity, Sukhi has been doing the same with femininity. Because we have three boys, our inquiry into child-rearing research leans toward the masculine, but the development of young women is equally important. It's our job, as members of a community, to create opportunities that expand the consciousness of all young people so they can develop self-confidence and find their places in the world.

Explore your own conditioning and how it creates your experience. Right now, you may or may not be aware of the walls you've built up. We all have them, and it's a continuous practice to let those walls come down and allow ourselves to be seen.

THE NERVOUS SYSTEM

As we start to understand our emotions, we need to understand a bit about the system that regulates them: our nervous system. After a lifetime of trauma and challenges, most of us have dysregulated nervous systems. Yet, we can very quickly learn to regulate our nervous systems, interrupt patterns of stress, and build our emotional resilience.

Our parasympathetic nervous system predominates in quiet "rest and digest" conditions, while the sympathetic nervous system drives the "fight, flight, or freeze" response in stressful situations. Our goal is to calm our sympathetic nervous system so that our parasympathetic nervous system can act more naturally and effectively.

First, it's important to notice how we react in various situations and what our default patterns and conditioned responses are. In times of stress, do you lean toward fight, flight, or freeze? We can operate in different ways depending on the circumstances, so take notice of what arises within you throughout the day.

Once we gain deeper awareness of our body's natural responses, we can activate tools to support ourselves in different circumstances.

One of the most powerful tools we can use is absolutely free and always accessible. It is an ancient tool that is often forgotten yet also growing in popularity: breathwork.

REST & DIGEST

- Calm, Relaxed, Open, Curious
- Constricted pupils
- Slow and deep breathing
- Decreased heart rate

FIGHT, FLIGHT, OR FREEZE

- Anger, Irriation, Worry
- Panic Disassociation
- Dilated pupils
- Increased breathing
- Accelerated heart rate

More and more research is being conducted to understand the power of breathwork on stress, anxiety, relaxation, energy, focus, sleep, and almost every other area of emotional well-being. Breathwork is a one-stop shop for parasympathetic support.

To start, take 5 to 10 minutes each day this week to do a conscious breathing exercise. Andrew Weil recommends a simple technique where you inhale to a count of four, hold to a count of seven, and then exhale to a count of eight. There are many apps you can try, such as *Breathwrk*, to guide you through "box" breathing and other techniques.

If you want to go one step further, the Oura Ring is an incredible wearable device that offers heart-rate monitoring, sleep analysis, guided breathing practices, and additional health insights to measure data around your nervous system. This is a powerful tool to take control over your well-being. In the interest of full disclosure, I am proud to have been an early investor in Oura and love using the product as much as I love working with the founders.

It has been incredible to watch the company use its research to improve quality of life. We are seeing firsthand how knowledge is power, and simply having the ability to track our biomarkers can support not only our physical health, but also our mental and emotional well-being. There is something powerful about receiving daily feedback on your "readiness" that enables you to make slight shifts in your day to support your overall health.

PHYSICAL WELL-BEING

Biohacking, also known as human augmentation or human enhancement, is aimed at improving physical well-being. The body is a temple; all of the signals and inputs it receives are interpreted by the physical vessel, and if the vessel is not optimized to receive signals in a way that supports our freedom, we become imprisoned.

The medical system is currently set up in a way that doesn't treat our bodies as the sacred vessels they are. Like many other systems in our society, healthcare is built from an economic standpoint, geared toward keeping investors and shareholders happy. Doctors are not taught to look for the root cause of health issues; rather, they focus on treating symptoms with medication.

Imagine a healthcare system that focuses more on time in nature, soaking in sunshine, cutting out processed foods, focusing on gut health, lowering stress, and getting daily physical activity and adequate vitamin D. We would achieve true sovereignty and freedom rather than rely solely on prescribed medications and interventions.

Using the concept of biohacking, each one of us can achieve physical freedom, purpose, and abundance. We can put ourselves in a position where we no longer rely on a system that doesn't have our best interests at heart. By looking at health through a new lens, we can regain control over our physical well-being. The following are key areas to explore to achieve physical freedom.

- **Diet:** Move toward eating an organic, whole-foods diet consisting mostly of vegetables, fruits, grass-fed meats, and healthy fats such as avocados and cold-pressed oils. Eliminate processed foods. Identify any allergies or sensitivities you may have.

- **Water:** Drink at least eight cups of clean, filtered water each day. Use a high-quality filter to avoid fluoride and other harmful chemicals that may be in the water system. The Berkey filter is the gold standard.

- **Light:** Soak in daily sunshine to build up vitamin D, and take a vitamin D3 supplement throughout the winter. Try out light therapy for added benefits.

- **Gut health:** The gut is the second brain. Test your gut microbiome to see where you can rebalance and implement more support. Viome.com has a test I recommend.

- **Sleep:** Get between seven and nine hours of sleep each night. Ensure you are getting adequate deep and rapid-eye-movement (REM) sleep as well. On the web, check out the Sleep Doctor for additional sleep resources. The Oura Ring is a great tool to keep track of the quality of your sleep.

- **Movement:** Moving your body is key to good health. Yoga is an amazing practice to bring into your life that supports your physical body, as well as your mental, emotional, and spiritual bodies. Even just 20 minutes of movement per day can make a massive impact.

- **Earthing:** Nature provides our bodies with so much nourishment. Take time to put your feet on the earth and just be outside. Earthing has been shown to reduce inflammation, pain, and stress, and to improve blood flow, sleep, and vitality.

The four elements of MEPS complement each other. As I was putting together this material, there were many times when I thought about a tool or technique that has an impact on several areas of well-being. In fact, there's one exercise that's quite physical and also vastly improves your mental and emotional well-being. If you have access to nature, find a spot in the forest that feels comfortable and allow your primal instincts to come out (safely, of course). This may feel uncomfortable at first. Scream at the top of your lungs. To move your kinetic energy, throw the largest log you can lift or kick your feet through the dirt. Scream even louder. Sing. Dance. Jump.

For some clues on why this exercise works, think about how children process their emotions. The process is not linear. At first, they misbehave a little and begin to push your buttons. This may escalate to using items, like throwing toys, pulling books off shelves, or creating a physical mess. Then perhaps they fall to the ground, screaming and pounding their fists. Finally, when all eardrums have been pierced, they slow down and cry.

The point I'm making is that as children, our bodies naturally know how to process emotions. Children do not allow emotions to lie dormant within until they bubble up and hurt themselves or others. Unfortunately, due to most adults' own conditioning, we do not know how to interact with children as they process emotions. We punish them or take love away from them until they "calm down" or "behave." This is what we also tell ourselves when emotions come up. It's a never-ending cycle unless we consciously choose to stop it.

So how *do* we stop it?

We rebuild safety in our lives to feel our emotions through our physical body. When I fully allow my anger to be felt and expressed (not at someone or myself but rather as a release into nature), the result is a cathartic and orgasmic experience. Once anger is fully released, it doesn't show up as passive aggressiveness or in other maladaptive ways to hurt myself or other people. As a result, it brings so much clarity of direction and freedom.

If you don't have access to a spot outside, your home will do (with a pillow for the screaming parts). Notice how you feel after your cathartic release.

Once you've moved your energy, you will feel a whole lot lighter. You may notice that the way you respond to other people changes and the unconscious ways you have learned to protect yourself slowly dissipate. For better physical well-being, here are four questions to continue asking:

1. How am I treating my physical body?

2. How can I upgrade my own biological operating system?

3. When did I last connect to nature and ground my feet on the earth?

4. Am I aware that the thoughts that I'm having are influencing the emotions I'm having, and that those emotions are influencing my physical health at this moment?

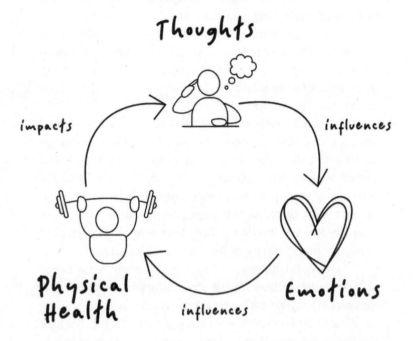

SPIRITUAL WELL-BEING

Spirituality is defined by the Oxford Dictionary as "the quality of being concerned with the human spirit or soul as opposed to material or physical things." While this is one of many possible definitions, it does a good job of outlining the transcendent and ethereal essence behind spirituality.

Many people compare spirituality to religion, but I see them as very different. Spirituality is not dogmatic. It is a way of living that is in connection to the spirit of all things.

When we examine spiritual freedom, we find a way of exploring the quality and depth of our relationship to self, each other, and nature. It's a way of living that is in alignment with the soul of all things.

The more you deepen your relationship with yourself, the more you will see yourself as interconnected with all beings in the natural world. When you see yourself as connected to all, rather than separate, it gives you the freedom to be yourself, because you know that you are a unique part of the collective, and that who you are intrinsically matters. This helps the collective grow and expand, and it helps us feel that we are just the universe experiencing and expanding itself through us. Instead of adhering to whom others want us to be, we become free to be who we are.

Remember that love is the basis of every spiritual practice. We must ensure that we are connected to our hearts. Then we can see ourselves as spirit itself, connected to all. This leads us to feeling more grateful.

Gratitude has miraculous effects on the mind, body, and emotions. It can improve cardiovascular health, inflammation, stress perception, diastolic blood pressure, and sleep. While the world around us may be chaotic, practicing gratitude each day can help us focus on the positive, supporting our physical well-being. Something you can start doing right away is making a gratitude list before bed each night.

Gratitude is the portal to experiencing more joy in life. It's that simple. When we express gratitude, we appreciate what we already have in our lives and make room for greater abundance. Robert Emmons, the world-leading scientific expert on the psychology of gratitude, found that not only does gratitude increase mental, emotional, and physical well-being, but it also impacts the overall experience of happiness and creates long-lasting effects.

Gratitude not only improves our immediate reality, but it also triggers positive feedback loops. When we experience gratitude, we feel more gratitude. This might seem obvious, but it's also easy to underestimate its power.

The gratitude produced in 10 minutes of intentional journaling can actually trigger a continuous grateful mood. While in that mood, we feel more gratitude longer and more often—that's a positive feedback loop.

Try it out. Through the simple act of journaling your gratitude or practicing gratitude meditations, you can shift your focus from what is lacking in your life to the abundance that already exists and is waiting to be cultivated.

Why do I keep pointing out what seems so obvious? Because cultivating gratitude is not something we do naturally. It's a learned behavior. With more practice, we can generate more positive feelings on demand.

Here's a simple way of practicing gratitude courtesy of James Clear, author of the best-selling book *Atomic Habits*: just say "thank you" more. Clear created a list of seven situations where you can say "thank you" more often:

Say "thank you"
when you're receiving a compliment.

Say "thank you"
when you're running late.

Say "thank you"
when you're comforting someone.

Say "thank you"
when you're receiving helpful feedback.

Say "thank you"
when you're receiving unfair criticism.

Say "thank you"
when someone gives you unsolicited advice.

Say "thank you" when you're not sure if you
should thank someone.[6]

When you read this list, you may wonder why you
would thank someone who criticizes you. For starters, we
are looking to make gratitude a habit. Having an auto-
matic response to say "thank you" puts you in a state of
gratitude. That creates a shift in your nervous system,
which will shape your perception. The moment after you
say "thank you," you just might realize that what seemed
like criticism was actually someone's way of trying to
help you improve. Or maybe you can smile and say to
yourself, "Yeah, thank you for reminding me to choose
more supportive friends!" Either way, your grateful state
changes your thoughts, and your well-being improves.

Another way to measure your total well-being is to
practice regulating your heart coherence. Coherence is an
important concept in areas like quantum physics, biology, and social science. When we are in coherence, the
different parts of our system are connected and work well
together. There are various types of coherence.

One example is physiological coherence, which can be
measured by looking at heart rate variability (HRV). HRV is
a measure of the variation in time between each heartbeat.
Scientists believe HRV offers a potentially noninvasive

way to understand our own nervous system. Based on collected data, a person in fight-or-flight will tend to experience lower variation in HRV—in other words, they'll experience shorter spaces between heartbeats. If a person is in a relaxed, parasympathetic state, they'll tend to experience longer spaces between heartbeats—they're in coherence.[7] HeartMath, the leading institution studying heart coherence, has done many studies have shown coherence can become disordered when we experience prolonged or intense amounts of stress or health problems.[8] In good health, our heart rhythms are smooth and steady, but they can become irregular when we're stressed or sick. These heart rhythms play a crucial role in how our body systems, including the brain, communicate with each other. When we are in a state of heart coherence, our body and mind fare better in terms of health, wellness, and performance. This can lead to a variety of benefits, including reduced stress and anxiety, improved mental clarity, and enhanced physical health.[9]

HeartMath research has discovered many ways our heart communicates with our body, such as through energy, electromagnetic fields, chemicals, and hormones. They have also developed practical methods for stress reduction, health improvement, and better performance. Additionally, they created biofeedback technology that helps people train their HRV to achieve more balanced heart rhythms.

Many spiritual traditions view the heart as the center of the soul, the place where we connect with our true selves and higher consciousness. Practicing heart coherence can help us tap into this deeper wisdom, leading to a greater sense of purpose and connection to something larger than ourselves. This feeling of harmony is often thought of as being "in the zone," or in flow.

Social coherence focuses on how people can have strong and peaceful relationships and build connection in pairs, families, small groups, or big organizations that have shared goals and interests. This requires group members to be emotionally connected and manage the group's feelings together. Several studies have shown that when people's body rhythms sync up, they are more likely to cooperate, trust, and care for each other.[10]

For better spiritual well-being, here are four questions to continue asking:

1. What is my relationship to myself, others, and nature?

2. What is my purpose?

3. Am I in the presence of gratitude?

4. Am I in the presence of love?

Once you integrate all four areas of MEPS, you will undoubtedly feel a shift in your mental, emotional, physical, and spiritual well-being.

CHAPTER 3 POWER PLAYS

M=Mental / E=Emotional / P=Physical / S=Spiritual

- ❏ **(M)** Look at the last 10 people you talked to, the last 10 people you texted, and the last 20 social media messages you read. Notice any themes in the types of messaging you are receiving and taking in, and whether discernment is needed within these conversations.

- ❏ **(E)** Read a book about trauma and processing emotions.

- ❏ **(E)** Download a breathing app and commit to a breathwork exercise each day for a week. Reflect on how you feel after one week of consistent, conscious breathwork, and make an effort to do it every day going forward.

- ❏ **(E)** Journal or share with a loved one a gratitude list each day this week.

- ❏ **(P)** Choose two to three biohacks (diet, water, gut health, light, sleep, movement, earthing) to focus on this week. Keep track of your progress on a calendar or in your journal.

- ❏ **(P/M/E)** Find a safe and private spot in nature or at home to kinetically move through emotions. Scream at the top of your lungs, throw the largest log you can lift, kick your feet through the dirt, scream even louder, sing, dance, and jump. Notice how you feel after moving emotions in this way.

- ❏ **(S)** Consider your relationship to masculine and feminine energy, and how you can cultivate a spiritual connection in your relationships.

4

FIND YOUR MISSION TO MARS

*When you realize there is nothing lacking,
the whole world belongs to you.*

— **LAO TZU**

While tech billionaires are building rockets to get to Mars, I discovered another MARS that I would like to invite you to. This MARS is a planet where Multiple Automated Revenue Streams abound.

By now, you have started the work to discover your purpose and improve your MEPS well-being. If you're consciously improving your mental, emotional, physical, and spiritual well-being, then your thoughts and emotions will be better regulated, and you'll be more physically and spiritually in tune with what's going on around you. Upgrades to your MEPS will help you to tune in to impact, wealth, and abundance. The opposite is true, too—if your operating system is dysregulated, if you're out of attunement with yourself and the world around you, or if you're operating from a place of survival, it will be difficult to operate at your highest possible level. Generating abundance is a byproduct of your ability to focus on those four areas of your life—and your ability to define your "Mission to MARS." In this chapter, we're going to redefine how you work, live, and play. Creating revenue with less effort will provide you the opportunity to design life on your own terms.

Many of us have been raised to believe that we need to go to college and get a job to support us for the rest of our lives. Unfortunately, we are not taught how we may end up enslaved by a system that doesn't care about our freedom.

Our current society is set up as a win-lose scenario. War, resource extraction, and cheap labor have become synonymous with modern-day capitalism. Perhaps you have felt your conscience kick in while shopping at Walmart or Amazon, knowing there is a child suffering on the other side of the bargains. However, even with this knowledge, millions of people shop there. To do so, they must disconnect from reality and choose not to see the impact of their purchases. On a grand scale, the cause-and-effect scenario is much greater than we ever imagined.

Our current economic system too often relies on extractive capitalism. For there to be a gain in value under capitalism, extraction must occur—either from humans extracting from other humans, or, more often, humans extracting from nature. If we don't raise our collective consciousness faster than the rate at which these exponential technologies are being developed, they will use us instead of us using them. Before we get to that dire point, we have the power to take responsibility for our capital and to powerfully coexist with not only humanity, but also with all life forms that Mother Nature has gifted us with. Shifting from a fear-based paradigm to a love-based paradigm is part of that process.

Whether you're in the role of consumer, employee, business owner, or investor, understanding that money is energy and how it is deployed has far-reaching ramifications. If we remain stuck in the old win-lose paradigm, we will continue to overlook the effect money has on our state of consciousness. If we move toward "conscious capital" on our journey to MARS, aware of where and how our money can improve our global state of consciousness, we can make decisions that support our highest good.

I believe Robert Kiyosaki's *Rich Dad, Poor Dad* became such a worldwide phenomenon (with more than 44 million copies sold[1] in over 40 languages)[2] because it helped wake people up from a false paradigm. Getting good grades and depending on the system—the Matrix—has never been a formula for anything but a grind. Meanwhile, acquiring skills and assets that generate recurring revenue has always been the path to wealth.

My "rich dad" is a guy named Andrew. You may remember that I attended a goal-setting event with him. Even though Andrew was an ordained monk, he also had success as a high-profile lawyer, music producer, biohacker, investor, and three-time unicorn builder. One of the secrets he taught me was how he applied the principle of compound interest.

Compound interest means earning interest on the principal balance and also earning interest on the interest. It's the multiplier effect, which quickly accelerates the growth of your savings and investments over time. It's no wonder that Albert Einstein said, "Compound interest is the eighth wonder of the world. He who understands it, earns it; he who doesn't, pays it."

What Andrew really instilled in me was the idea of *compound thoughts*. Just as fear can spiral, amazing ideas can spiral as well. When you allow them to build upon each other, magic unfolds. Compound thoughts, like compound interest, lead to less effort and more impact. It reminds us that when we work smarter, we have more time to play and create abundance.

The old paradigm is built on the thought that we first need to make a lot of money to live the life we want, and then we'll have space to focus on our MEPS. Too many of us have said, too many times, that "I'll make an impact when . . ." *When* I finish law school, *when* the kids start school, *when* we go public, etc. We wait for an external factor to create that safety net, and we think we have to

reach some prerequisite before we can live a fulfilled life and make an impact. This thinking only perpetuates our own suffering (working and living with no purpose while waiting for *x* to happen). It's like driving with one foot on the gas and one on the brake, yet still hoping to reach our destination. This can be summed up with the phrase, "Have, Do, Be," or the mindset of "When I have more _____ , I'll be able to do _____ , so I can be [happy, fulfilled, healthy, etc.]."

But instead of thinking that you need to achieve something first so you can be a certain way, you can simply decide to *be* who you want now. In doing so, you'll be guided to *do* what resonates and will *have* plenty of abundance.

We want to operate from the new paradigm of "Be, Do, Have." The essence of it is this: "I'm going to be happy and do the things that give me purpose, so I can have a meaningful life."

As New Millionaires, we see abundance differently. Our goal is to reach a place where our investments directly correlate with our state of consciousness. We are focused on creating self-sufficiency and building resources to break free from the Matrix and create our own financial blueprint. Having multiple streams of income is a result of living our purpose and positively impacting the world. In doing so, we can reach a state of awareness that gives us the power to tap into our greater wisdom to change the energetic value of money.

CREATING ABUNDANCE

Financial abundance means we not only have the physical resources needed to thrive, but also that our quality of life is in alignment with our highest selves. It means having the freedom to go where we want to go, do what we want to do, and be who we want to be.

Your relationship to money and abundance is a direct reflection of how you relate to yourself. If you relate to yourself through scarcity—*I don't have enough time, I don't know enough, I'm not good enough*—that's the same energy and frequency that you'll bring to your money and everything else in your life. Remember, the most important currency you have is your thoughts. If your thoughts are consistently poor, how do you expect to create abundance?

When you start relating to yourself as generous, abundant, infinite, and resourceful, then your relationship to wealth will change. It's easier to see yourself as in control of your own destiny, rather than a cog in the wheel or a victim of circumstances.

Let's be clear, though: the point of success is not money but impact. If you begin to see yourself as someone who can create maximum impact, you'll also begin to see the connection between impact and abundance. When you bring in money as the result of making the biggest and most positive impact on people, you open up channels and connections to abundance.

Connecting to abundance channels is like working with the qi of the body. When you unblock those channels, things just flow. Multiple Automated Revenue Streams (MARS) are a part of that flow. When you build a business or income stream out of a desire to make an impact, you become aligned to a higher frequency. It's that impact that builds your sense of purpose and self-worth, while money builds your sense of abundance.

If you're not feeling aligned with the idea of the flow of abundance, this creates an opportunity for reflection. Ask yourself the following questions:

- How am I co-creating this block to abundance?

- Where do I need to look to understand this?

- Where am I not loving myself?

- What mental models or underlying programming do I have that makes me believe I'm not worthy of abundance, and where did that come from (childhood, current friends, etc.)?

- Say this statement out loud: "I am worthy of abundance." Notice where you feel constriction in your body in response to these words. Talk to that part of your body, and ask gentle questions to get to the heart of the constriction. Why is it there, and what is it trying to tell you?

This all comes back to self-worth. If you believe you're not worthy or not good enough, it's no surprise that you feel an abundance block. In that case, you might also believe that you just have to work harder or hustle harder to get the abundance you want.

The quantum leap available to you is the belief that you are worthy. It's not about working harder or hustling harder—you are worthy of abundance, no matter where you are in life right now. You are a beautiful soul, a light-filled being, who is worthy of all of the experiences in life you desire.

CREATE YOUR VISION

To start, I invite you to take a blank piece of paper and draw an image of pure possibility that represents what you want to create in the world. Let this be a sort of vision board where you can see everything you are calling in. Use paint, pens, colored pencils, images from magazines—the sky's the limit. If you prefer to keep your vision board digital, use web or phone-based apps to create it. Draw in as many of the elements from your work in Chapter 2 as you can. This vision should serve as a representation of the possibilities you see for your life, starting right now.

Now do the following exercise:

- Create an inventory of where you are now in relation to your dream.

  1. What parts of your dream feel like they're just within reach?

  2. Which parts of your dream feel harder to attain or like they might take years to achieve?

  3. What are the clear steps you can take to get closer to your dream?

- How aligned are you with your current mode of making money?

  1. Does your work make a positive impact?

  2. Do you feel a sense of integrity in your work?

- What would it look like to be truly proud of how you make your living?

- How much money do you need to make to serve your future vision?

Describe exactly what an abundant life looks like to you. Be as specific as possible. Where are you living? What kind of home(s) do you have? Who is around you? How are you spending your time? What hobbies are you pursuing? How much money are you generating?

So many people have the belief that they need millions of dollars to live their dream, when it's likely they don't need that much at all. The new millionaire doesn't bank on the idea that they can live their life once they have all of the money they need. The new millionaire lives their life now and brings in what they need with effortless flow. Get clear on where you are in relation to that vision so you can build your MARS to help you bring that to life.

In addition to considering how we earn money, let's also think about how we spend it—and make sure both are aligned with our highest values. Some of us are stuck in the loop of consumerism, grinding to make money and then spending it on things we think will make us happy, without truly examining what that means. To make choices that align with the life we desire, we must first clarify our desires.

Creating this vision is the first step in actualizing it. Once you've come up with your list, describe how you will feel once you have all of those things. Use the present tense, and as you write out each feeling, breathe into the emotion and allow the feeling of abundance to move through your body. Here are some examples:

- I feel a sense of peace and calm each day.
- I feel deeply loved by the people around me.
- I feel immense gratitude for my life.
- I feel joy and lightheartedness.
- I feel aligned with my purpose.

Tuning in to these feelings will help you facilitate your journey to MARS.

Once you have created your vision board of possibilities, choose a like-minded friend to share it with. Intention is more powerful when shared, so take the opportunity to speak your dreams into reality. Keep your vision board somewhere you can see it often, and continue to take actionable steps from this book to help bring it into reality.

MEPS WELL-BEING LEADS TO MARS

My friend Alecia is a teacher and identifies as a technophobe. Though she loves her job and feels fulfilled working with children, the stressful nature of her job was leading to burnout. After work, Alecia liked to zone out with a few glasses of prosecco and reruns of *The Office*. When schools shut down during the pandemic, dozens of parents reached out to her. The gist of their comments was, "I wish I had the tools I needed to support my kids at home. I just feel so lost and stressed trying to do what you do."

Her initial internal response was, *You think you have problems? The last thing I need is to hear more complaints from parents.*

When Alecia vented to me, I listened and gave her the space to share her thoughts. On top of validating her experience, I shared with her that I sensed the cause of her frustration was overextending herself for others without first taking care of herself. I suggested that she spend some time in nature and journal about what still brought her joy and excitement around her work.

Alecia returned to taking walks and journaling. She shared with me a list she had written that included points like these:

- Seeing the excitement on a child's face when they learn something new

- Helping parents deepen their relationship with their kids through fun games and exercises

- Coordinating activities for students that are creative and surprising

- Sharing best practices so my ideas can be used by others

A few days later, Alecia's sister, who was also struggling with homeschooling, suggested that she turn this "problem" into an opportunity. Her idea was for Alecia to put together and sell a short guide for parents to equip their homes for homeschooling. Alecia's initial reaction was that it sounded like a lot of work. When she ran it by me, confessing how intimidated she was about anything tech related, I referred her to a friend who could handle that part for her.

Over the weekend, Alecia started creating a written guide and soon found herself in a flow state. She had great ideas, and it lit her up to know that sharing them could help so many people. Before long, she had completed a 12-page guide. Then she leveraged the power of technology to create an automated revenue stream. She worked with my friend to upload it to a website, used Zapier to enhance a simple funnel, and shared the link with parents. Word spread because she had solved a problem! This is an example of ikigai in action: the money poured in.

Alecia's success with this one simple product led her to create additional guides that solved other problems that parents have. The revenue gave her what so many of us crave—choices! With so many more options available to her, Alecia considered teaching part time and exploring exciting and enriching ways to support parents and children. It also allowed her to double her tutoring rate and be even more selective in choosing clients. As her tutoring business moved online and her guides kept generating revenue, she booked a trip to Costa Rica. Though she wasn't sure if she wanted to be a digital nomad, she felt freedom knowing that she could be. The words *holistic* and *well-being* are often overused, but Alecia is an example of how both led to creating abundance. Alecia first had to regulate her nervous system and change her perception to put herself in a receptive place. She also had to embrace technology, which, for her, meant hiring someone else to handle it. In doing so, she created an automated revenue stream that was aligned with her purpose.

Let's unpack Alecia's story. Alecia felt a deep sense of purpose around helping children learn. She also has a lot of skills in this area, given her work as a teacher. When opportunity in the form of a pandemic appeared, she knew she could fulfill a need for other people. She created something amazing that meets that need, and she automated the sale and delivery of it. Now she sees tons of new possibility for her life. This is an amazing example of using MARS to change your life. Most people respond to stress by feeling overwhelmed. New Millionaires like Alecia, on the other hand, develop an uncanny knack for turning stress into opportunities. That's the alchemy of a Conscious Thought Revolution.

You have spent the time to fall in love with your brain and discover your unique purpose. In doing so, you have discovered clues to generate multiple revenue streams. The process of generation, though, is highly personal. Others will tell you (or try to sell you) why their strategy is the best. This is yet another reason to stay off Instagram! For example, I could suggest that you build an online course to make money, but if that would create more frustration than flow for you, it wouldn't make sense.

When you consider how you're going to create your MARS, ask yourself what falls within your zone of genius and solves a problem for someone else. Keep asking: What problems are you uniquely suited to solve? How are other people struggling with MEPS well-being? If you are able to create a solution to a common problem, you may have found a business or at least one solid revenue stream.

When you think of or hear about an idea, pay attention to your reaction. If, for every idea, your initial response tends to be, *I can't do that*, you are likely coming from a place of fear. Ask yourself, *Why am I thinking that thought?*

What would it feel like to have multiple automated revenue streams as a part of your everyday life? And how might it be fun and playful to discover those revenue streams? It wasn't that long ago that market research was reserved for big companies with massive budgets. Now you can easily post on social media or send an email to friends and ask for quick feedback. Think about the people you know who already ask you about things like gardening, baking, tech support, or website design. Figure out how to solve a problem and create one simple product that will make people's lives better, and you are on your way to creating an automated revenue stream.

The next phase is to quickly test your ideas. *Minimum viable product* (MVP) is more than the title of the pilot episode for the TV series *Silicon Valley*. It's a term used to describe creating a product with a minimal investment that allows you to gather feedback before moving on to the next stage. This is where we get to reframe the way we think about social media and how we can use it instead of it using us. Through social media, you have access to millions of people at your fingertips. Instead of doomscrolling, think about how to leverage your access to social media to build your revenue streams. Between asking targeted questions and gathering information on social media, you have the ability to constantly test your ideas for revenue streams. The book *The Lean Startup*, by Eric Ries, is also a great resource.

Do you see how the Keys work together and why you first need to unplug from the Matrix? Your thoughts, particularly around abundance, will impact your perception of what is possible. Before you decide that you can't afford a down payment on a house or land, consider that in some situations, it's possible to buy property with the help of local and federal loans and grants, or to apply for special funding with a local community credit union.

Remember that Key #2 is discovering your purpose. Now is the perfect time to go back to your curiosity list, your vision board, and your list of 15 problems in the world you would like to see solved. And as you witnessed from Alecia's story, focusing on MEPS well-being is also a great source of ideas.

THE ROLES OF TECHNOLOGY

The next 10 years will be like no other in the history of humanity. Technology is evolving at the speed of light.

The very fabric of our existence is going to change because of exponentially emerging technologies. Machine learning and quantum computing will allow us to calculate the incalculable. Meanwhile, blockchain technology, decentralized ledger technology, and cryptocurrency are all changing the money game.

Let's define exponential technology. Exponential technology refers to technologies that grow and improve at an accelerating rate, far beyond what we would expect from linear growth. Think of artificial intelligence (AI), augmented and virtual reality (AR and VR), digital biology, data science, medical tech, nanotech, robotics, and autonomous vehicles. As these technologies advance, they create new opportunities and capabilities that further accelerate their growth.

The development of the Internet and mobile technology has enabled the creation of powerful new tools such as artificial intelligence, cloud computing, and blockchain technology. Each of these technologies has in turn created new industries, products, and services that are transforming the ways we live and work.

What distinguishes exponential technologies from traditional technologies is their ability to amplify their own capabilities through feedback loops, network effects, and rapid iteration, creating a virtuous cycle of growth and innovation that can lead to disruptive changes in society and the economy.

To get a better understanding of the power of exponential technologies, let's look at the concept of ephemeralization, which was introduced by Buckminster Fuller. *Ephemeralization* refers to the ability of technology to do more and more with less and less until eventually you can do everything with nothing.[3] Essentially, ephemeralization is the idea that technology can become increasingly efficient and effective over time, allowing us to achieve more using fewer resources.

Fuller believed that ephemeralization was a natural progression of technological development, driven by human ingenuity and innovation. He argued that as we develop more advanced technologies, we will be able to create more efficient and effective systems that require fewer resources to run. This, in turn, allows us to do more with less, ultimately leading to a world where we can achieve almost anything without the need for significant material resources.

Fuller saw ephemeralization as a solution to many of the world's problems, including poverty, resource depletion, and environmental degradation. By developing technologies that can do more with less, we can create a more sustainable and equitable world that meets the needs of all people without sacrificing the planet's natural resources.

Further to that point, Ray Kurzweil, one of the world's leading inventors, said, "Our intuition about the future is linear. But the reality of information technology is exponential, and that makes a profound difference. If I take 30 steps linearly, I get to 30. If I take 30 steps exponentially, I get to a billion."[4]

Exponential thinking applies to the way we approach making a positive impact on the world. We've often talked about our ability to impact millions of people, but you don't have to actually reach 1 million people on your own. Even if you positively affect the lives of just 100 or 1,000 people, the ripple effect of these relationships built on trust, authenticity, and integrity can be incredible. This idea is powerful because it speaks to the virality of positive impact and the importance of critical mass. When you use the incredible technology we have today, it's not as daunting as it may sound.

With the technologies available, you have the opportunity to grow your revenue streams exponentially. Using AI has the potential to revolutionize the way you build your MARS. When you leverage machine-learning algorithms, it becomes easy to automate routine tasks and decision-making processes, freeing up your time and energy to focus on more creative and strategic ideas. AI can help you identify new opportunities, analyze vast amounts of data in real time, and optimize operations for maximum efficiency and profitability. Additionally, AI can help you personalize your offerings to better meet the needs of customers, which leads to greater customer satisfaction and loyalty. The use of AI in business has the potential to streamline operations, increase productivity, and ultimately drive the growth of abundance, making it an indispensable tool for every one of us. In the future, there will be two kinds of companies: those that use AI and those that fail.

Because of quantum computing and artificial intelligence, all the world's information is available in a way that it never has been before. That means that all of the thinking and knowledge out there now can be put to use in your specific scenario. This is incredible—every single business owner now has an advantage that they've never had before. So much of the work of building a business can be done at the snap of a finger, enabling you to spend more time doing things you love.

When I talk about Web3 or blockchain, eyes glaze over. Many people tune out because they don't know how it works. But consider this—do you send an e-mail every day? I'm guessing the answer is yes. Could you tell me how email or the Internet works? I'm guessing not. When you signed up for your first email address, you probably didn't know (or care) how the ISP works and how many packets were exchanged. It didn't matter to you because it still worked whether you "got it" or not.

Similarly, it doesn't matter if you fully understand how AI or any of these technologies work. It only matters that you start participating and get in the game. In truth, everyone is already using many of these technologies and have been using it for years. If you've ever used Siri or Alexa, you've used AI. If you've shopped with Amazon's suggestion feed, you've used AI. The question isn't whether to use it; the question is how you're going to use it to build the life you want.

I've said a lot about using AI and online technology to build a business, but I don't want you to get the impression that all of your revenue streams must be digital. Let's say part of your purpose is to heal through touch. That's wonderful—and at the same time, there will be an upper limit as to how much you can charge and how many sessions a day you can have. However, you can still use AI to build this business into an automated revenue stream. You can use AI to build a website, drive traffic, get leads, and systematize processes that make it easy for customers to sign up for sessions. Eventually you might decide that you're ready to teach part of your healing work, so you could record videos, turn that into an online class, and sell that program—all through automated systems. Already, it's possible to set up a business in less than a day.

The point here isn't that everything you do should be online, but that everything you do can be made easier and as automated as it can be so that you no longer have to trade time for money. Automation not only makes it easier to run your business, but it frees you up to have more time to build other revenue streams—which means you'll never be dependent on any one stream. That alone will give you the freedom to make choices on your own terms.

Your revenue streams can reflect all of the different expressions of your purpose. You might have a super techy side that loves being at the forefront of technology. You might also have a side that likes to cook and wants to open a micro-bakery, work that's tied to the material world. You can live out both of these expressions; just be sure that you're always looking for opportunities to automate and simplify.

THE ROLE OF CRYPTOCURRENCY

We are entering an era where more and more of our existence will be digitalized. So much of our life happens in the digital world already, but there will be more to come, and money will change, too. It's estimated that by 2030 we'll live in a cashless society.[5] Whatever you do, I want you to think about how cryptocurrency might play into your revenue streams now and in the future.

Crypto is not issued by a central authority, meaning it cannot be influenced by government interference or manipulation. Crypto takes the power away from a central authority and puts it into the people's hands. It is programmable money for which the community creates the rules and principles through smart contracts. This is why cryptocurrency is growing and is only getting bigger. At the same time, crypto is highly volatile and requires specific knowledge and understanding to safely trade and store. The learning curve can feel steep, which is why many people have avoided it. Because the opportunity is so great, it is vitally important to become familiar with it.

What the Internet did for the transparency of information, blockchain will do for the transparency of money. Right now, if you make an investment in a company that claims it is socially positive, you can't see where your money is going, and therefore you can't accurately measure the effectiveness of your investment. But that's changing, thanks to blockchain.

Blockchain, the foundation on which crypto sits, is a distributed ledger technology (DLT) that consists of a growing list of records (blocks) that are securely linked together across an entire network of computer systems on the blockchain. This way of recording information makes it nearly impossible to change, hack, or cheat the system. Each block contains information about the block previous to it, including a timestamp and transaction data.

You don't need to understand the nuances of the underlying technology of the blockchain to invest in crypto. Don't let that hold you back; otherwise you will be late to the party. You simply need to know that it creates a revolutionary way of moving money and information. The quantum leap here is to simply get into the game. To see how easy it is to invest in crypto, visit newmillionaires playbook.com.

Crypto is a major part of the growing metaverse. The metaverse is the driving force bringing Web3, digital currency, and blockchain technologies together in a unified, immersive experience. There's a reason Facebook changed its name to Meta. Zuckerberg and his team aren't the only ones betting big on building an entire ecosystem in the metaverse. Even though the metaverse is still nascent in terms of its usability, it's hard to ignore the impact. Much like AI, you might think you're not familiar with the metaverse. But if you have kids, or know someone who plays video games—which, by the way, is a $37 billion industry predicted to grow to a $663 billion industry by 2030—then you're already exposed to the metaverse.[6]

This type of talk was once reserved for futurists. Now the future is here. According to *Forbes*:

> Metaverse real estate (or should that be virtual estate?) is already big business. Superstars, including Snoop Dogg, and global businesses, including PwC, JP Morgan, HSBC, and Samsung, have already snapped up plots of virtual land, which they intend to develop for a variety of purposes. Those who got in early have already made big returns—on paper, at least. In late 2021, the average price for the smallest plot of land available to buy on Decentraland or the Sandbox—two of the biggest metaverse platforms—was under $1,000. Today it's sitting at around $13,000.[7]

Imagine a new city being built. Construction companies and anyone who can build infrastructure would be looking at a windfall. Now imagine an entire new universe being built! As unbelievable as it sounds, demand for real estate in the metaverse has been skyrocketing—and it's difficult to buy without cryptocurrency.

This is beyond a gold rush. According to J.P. Morgan, "The metaverse will likely infiltrate every sector in some way in the coming years, with the market opportunity estimated at over $1 trillion in yearly revenues . . . In-game ad spending is set to reach $18.41 billion by 2027."[8]

Opportunities are there for anyone with curiosity and consciousness. A concert held in the game *Fortnite* grossed

$20 million in revenue because it was viewed by 45 million people. What does this have to do with MARS? That depends on your interest, skills, and statement of purpose. If you know how to create incredible experiences, imagine what you can do when not constrained by barriers such as the capacity of a venue.

I know the technological possibilities can be daunting; however, it's hard to ignore the excitement created by these innovations. As long as you stay conscious, you'll find your own path to MARS. The goal is to feel empowered and in control of your financial freedom. The choice is yours—remain a slave to the system that is built on greed and power, or choose a new way forward. Each has its fair share of challenges. Only one will set you free.

CHAPTER 4 POWER PLAYS

❏ Describe in writing what your most abundant life looks like. Then write how you will feel when you are living your most abundant life. Create a vision board that captures the essence of your dream. Use paint, markers, and magazines, or if you prefer a digital version, use a web or phone app.

❏ Examine how you currently spend your money. Notice if it is not in alignment with your values, and, if not, shift it.

❏ Complete your Mission to MARS.
  1. Make a list of all your current revenue streams.
  2. If you are employed, ask for a raise.
  3. Brainstorm all other ways to achieve MARS.

❏ Review different automated revenue streams and decide which you can comfortably tap into right now.

❏ Set up a crypto wallet and invest your first $50 in cryptocurrency.

5

BUILD RESILIENCE, RESOURCES, AND RELATIONSHIPS

Two roads diverged in a wood and I—
I took the one less traveled by,
And that has made all the difference.

— **ROBERT FROST**

A young woman from Canada named Ashley fought peer pressure from society to go to university. Rather than spend time in a classroom, pursuing a degree that didn't really interest her, she decided to solo travel, learning more about herself, the world, and how she desired to live. Ashley used sites such as Workaway and WWOOF to find volunteer and work opportunities abroad where she could expand her skills, meet new people, and live life on her own terms.

When fighting the status quo, some of us look for ways to work within the system. The term *gap year* may have been invented by curious souls who wanted to explore life while keeping their peers, parents, and guidance counselors at bay.

One such opportunity led Ashley to Vancouver Island and an organic farm called Ravenhill Herb Farm, run by my friends Todd and Brea. Ashley specifically chose this farm because Todd and Brea also happened to be partners in Pacific Rim College, which offers programs in holistic medicine and sustainable living, and she knew she could learn a lot from them. At the time, I was looking for an executive assistant. When I next saw Todd and Brea, they couldn't stop talking about Ashley—her attitude, work ethic, infectious energy, and ability to get shit done.

I didn't ask to see her resume. I didn't care where, or if, she went to college. It was my relationship with my friends—and their glowing appraisal of her—that led me to want to meet her. When we hopped on a video call, it took all of about two minutes to know I wanted her on my team. I used tools such as the Kolbe score to see how she worked, and asked more potent questions than "What are your strengths and weaknesses?" I tasked her with a small project to get attuned to how she works and used all of these relationship-building skills to ensure it was the right fit.

That was over five years ago. Ashley's contribution has been so beyond definition that we simply call her the "Creatrix of Possibilities." The traits that Ashley innately had—being growth-oriented, curious, inquisitive, and optimistic—made her a person I wanted to invest time, resources, and energy into. Ashley's drive to take the uncharted paths made her a New Millionaire at a much younger age than I was.

As we dive into this Key, keep in mind that as much as people try to convince us that the traditional path is the safe path, *real freedom and safety comes from finding your own way.* You don't build resilience by living somebody else's life. You also can't do it alone.

Working with Ashley has been a core reminder of the importance of resilience, relationships, and resources— and how they all work together. When we break out of the paradigm of *how much can this person do for me?,* and instead approach relationships from a place of reciprocity, we see how much more we can actually receive and how much better we can set ourselves up for turbulent times.

Understand that as much as people try to convince us that the traditional path is the safe path, *real freedom and safety comes from finding your own way.* You don't build resilience by living somebody else's life—and you don't do it alone. You may know the story of Margaret Mead. When asked what she considered to be the first sign of civilization in a culture, she replied that it was a femur that had been broken and then healed. That wouldn't have happened in the animal kingdom, where a broken leg means certain death. Mead reportedly said that a "broken femur that has healed is evidence that someone has taken time to stay with the one who fell, has bound up the wound, has carried the person to safety and has tended the person through recovery. Helping someone else through difficulty is where civilization starts."[1]

Real freedom and safety comes from finding your own way.

That's why we're going to talk about the people we love and how we design freedom to deepen our relationships and increase our chances of survival during uncertain times.

BUILDING RESILIENCE

If there's one thing that COVID-19 taught us, it's that you can never have enough toilet paper. While the thought is pretty comical, we all experienced how chaos and uncertainty spread fear. During the pandemic, the importance of being prepared for any sort of disaster suddenly felt a lot more real.

Resilience is a crucial quality for all of us to cultivate before—and during—stressful and chaotic situations. Resilience isn't limited to individuals; however, it's just as important that organizations, communities, and nations develop it too. In today's interconnected world, global events like geopolitical instability, pandemics, economic shocks, and climate change can have a significant impact on local communities and the people who live and work in them, making resilience even more critical. By cultivating resilience, we can better equip ourselves to overcome these challenges and persevere.

Right now is an opportunity to reflect on what is most important in your life—and take steps to protect it. If the world as you know it changed tomorrow, what would you need to continue to survive? Where would you want to live? What access would you have to food and water? Who would you want around you? These are some of the questions to keep in mind and continue to reflect on as we move toward our quest for physical freedom.

This is a moment in history when anything that is out of alignment will not survive. We are dismantling systems that no longer serve us in order to pave a new path forward. This is in response to uncovering previously hidden mistruths.

The current financial system is going through an evolutionary shift. Wall Street and Washington may try to convince us that this is an ordinary economic cycle and we should pour our money into the stock market. The United States printed more money between 2020 and 2023 than it did in the previous 100 years. Inflation rose to its highest level in more than four decades. Governments and central banks can try to tinker with the system, raising and lowering interest rates, but they are out of answers when the system is broken. Stay dependent on such a system at your own peril.

We can move our money out of banks and explore other streams of financial security that are not in the hands of an unstable economy. Having more than one passport is a prudent strategy if your circumstances fit the parameters of another country's passport requirements. That could mean applying for one in the country of your grandparents' origin or moving to a country where residency is easy to gain.

Whether this feels like something you need to do yesterday or something you aspire to, keep an open mind and focus on how you can create more independence and build a community that uplifts you and those around you.

Get out of *their* game and create your own.

The rich are getting richer, while more and more people are struggling to stay afloat. The disparity is immense. As Wall Street and private equity firms continue to buy residential real estate and gobble up land, the traditional notion that wealth is what you own and control is continuously reinforced. Bill Gates is the largest private owner of land in America, with more than 269,000 acres. There are clear parallels between the world's richest people and what they own.

I'm sharing this with one clear message: Get out of *their* game and create your own. The goal is to feel empowered and in control of your freedom.

HOW TO THINK ABOUT SURVIVAL

Human beings are obsessed with survival. We watch reality TV shows about it and create story lines centered around humanity's attempt to survive. This makes sense, as the most important thing in our human minds is survival. Even as the world has gotten safer in many ways, we are programmed to want to survive. Whether we like to think about it or not, most of us would do whatever it takes for self-preservation. It is a part of our DNA.

Still, most of us aren't prepared for a disaster. We have grown accustomed to security and safety in our lives and do not think in terms of worst-case scenarios. We trusted

EXTERNAL FACTORS

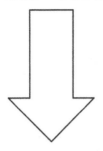

| Survival List, Self-defense & Security |
| Location, Supplies, Finances |
| Relationships & Community |
| Precious Metals |
| Food, Water, Permaculture |
| Regenerative Land & Real Estate |

RESILIENCE

that we would be taken care of by corporations, the government, or perhaps by our communities.

At least for me, that trust has shrunk to zero. The responsibility to keep my family safe and secure is 100 percent my own. I imagine you also feel the need to take safety and security into your own hands. Maybe you have thought about a worst-case scenario plan but aren't sure how to execute it.

Let's dive into a few questions that will help you assess where you are now and where you want to go. Take your time and work through them slowly. Work with a trusted neighbor, close friend, or family member to depend on one another for certain things. We are not meant to go through life alone. Having support from our community is incredibly important, especially in dire times.

Here are the most important categories to consider and prepare a survival plan around:

Location

- Is your location safe in the event of a crisis?

- Is there somewhere else you would prefer to live?

- Do you have access to land?

- If you live in the city, do you have a backup rural location you could go to if needed?

- Do you have community support around you?

- Do you have a second passport?

- How is your home protected from extreme weather conditions in your geographical location?

Food, Water, and Permaculture

- Do you have enough food to last you at least one to three months, including freeze-dried foods, frozen foods, and nonperishable goods?

- Are you able to grow your own food?

- Do you have enough fertilizer?

- Do you have enough water to last you for at least six months?

Supplies

- Do you have a generator in case the power goes out?

- Do you have a survival kit?

Finances

- Do you have $1K to $5K in cash securely stored in a safe at home?

- Do you have investments in real estate?

- Do you own gold and/or silver (some kept in vaults and some in your physical location)?

- Do you own cryptocurrency?

Self-Defense and Security

- Have you taken a self-defense course?

- Do you have the adequate tools to protect yourself?

- Do you have an anti-surveillance setup on your devices (i.e., DuckDuckGo, Proton Mail, a virtual private network [VPN])?

Food Guide

The top three recommendations for keeping an emergency food supply include: freeze-dried foods, frozen foods, and nonperishable goods. Each type of food has a different expiration, so it's good to have a combination of each and to update every six months. Based on your family size, the amount of food you store will differ. I recommend always having a food supply that can last at least three months.

I understand we're all at different phases in this journey. If buying land and raising goats seems unfathomable to you at this point in your life (or amazing yet intimidating), maybe join a community garden instead or grow herbs on your balcony. Whatever you do, start making progress and building momentum toward seeing yourself as a sovereign human being. One simple step to be less dependent on the system will make you feel more empowered.

REGENERATIVE LAND AND REAL ESTATE

Everyone needs somewhere to live. Putting your money into a home is a way to get your money out of the bank and have a physical place to create resilience. If current trends continue, the home will likely appreciate in value. You may find an opportunity to choose a lower-cost fixer-upper, especially if you're skilled with repairs and design, and make renovations to increase the value of the home.

Then again, depending on your situation, this may feel out of reach. Beyond the financials, psychologically, a 30-year commitment to a bank may feel like the antithesis of freedom. My best advice for young people is to have multiple roommates. Especially as rents have skyrocketed, it gives you a chance to build savings and relationships. You'll learn compassion and communication skills—while increasing your desire to create freedom and abundance.

Having property also secures physical freedom, providing retreat in times of need. Am I *telling* you to build a bunker? By now, I hope you see that I'm not *telling* you to do anything. I am, however, *asking* you to determine what you need to feel safe.

Buying raw land that you can build on may be a wise real estate investment. While it doesn't offer a shelter at first, it provides the flexibility to build what you desire, often at a much lower cost. There are so many affordable choices of exciting tiny homes, modular homes, and domes. You can buy something where you can grow your own food and feed off the land instead of depending on big-box grocery stores. Pre-pandemic, this sounded like paranoia. Now, it just sounds like the safest and smartest thing you can do for you and your family.

It doesn't have to be a 200-acre ranch. You don't need that much land to create food security. You can raise chickens on less than a third of an acre. The people who teased you at first will soon be the ones asking for eggs, especially given how much the price of eggs has skyrocketed.

Self-sufficiency is one of the most important investments of our time. This includes self-sufficient electricity generation, like solar panels, direct access to water (this factors into where you buy your land), and knowledge of permaculture. Regardless of the worst-case scenario, independence from broken systems for life's essentials is an extremely empowering and rewarding experience. Maybe as important, you create security for neighbors and loved ones.

Community living is becoming more appealing to many people. Buying shared land with others to build on can provide the financial and physical freedom you are looking for. If you have shied away from real estate because of the upfront costs, shared land is an option that may reduce your down payment. As you become more conscious, you'll be better suited to choose truly aligned partners.

RESILIENCE IS NOT A SOLO ENDEAVOR (COMMUNITY)

From the moment we are born, we look to the people around us to make sense of the world. Our parents or guardians are the first people we have relationships with, and they set us up on our life paths. Unfortunately, many of us did not have role models who were aware of their own conditioning, and as a result, they showed us a way of relational being that was unsupportive to our well-being.

After spending thousands of hours and countless dollars on various courses, technologies, and promises of leading a more fulfilled and happy life, I've come to learn and understand that human connection, or lack thereof, is a topic that comes up in *every single one of them*.

This isn't necessarily surprising. More and more studies show that neglect and lack of love in infancy lead to long-term mental health problems, as well as overall reduced potential and happiness.[2]

We are moving further away from our original way of being, which was to be raised in intergenerational communities. Every generation is struggling as a result. Children are not learning through multiage connections, parents are feeling more alone, and elders have no one to share their wisdom and knowledge with. Just imagine how different the world and our lives would be if we came back to a place of valuing connection as essential.

There are so many ways early relationships play out in our lives, but what we want to focus on is the people we choose to have in our lives now. When we clarify the types of people we want to surround ourselves with, we can understand more clearly how we see ourselves and our place in the world. In order to have true freedom, we have to ensure that our relationships are nourishing and supportive. There should be a reciprocal exchange of energy, a give and take; the goal is to have relationships that energize us rather than *drain* our energy.

Changing our relationship patterns is one of the most challenging things to do, because so much of our identity is tied to the people in our lives—our family, friends, and partners. It is scary to confront the fact that any or all of these relationships may not be working. For that reason, we will focus on the people you *want* in your life. From here, you can reassess your current relationships and create new ones that are truly in line with who you want to be.

GIVERS AND TAKERS

I shared earlier that as a child, I was adept at creating win-win situations. And even though everyone around me got what they wanted, my primary motivation was to get what I wanted. As I matured, I started to see this dynamic more clearly—and I saw that my relationships lacked depth and authenticity. I had a tendency to view my connections with others as a resource to use.

In his book *Give and Take*, Adam Grant posits that our success and happiness in life are not solely determined by our individual talent, hard work, or luck, but instead by the relationships we build with others. Grant identifies three types of people in the world: takers, matchers, and givers. Takers are people who primarily focus on getting as much as they can from others, often at the expense of others' well-being. Matchers believe in a quid-pro-quo approach, where they try to maintain a balance of giving and taking. Givers, on the other hand, are people who prioritize helping others, even if there's no immediate benefit to themselves. Givers are often the most successful and fulfilled people in life. They are more likely to build strong and meaningful relationships, gain trust and respect from others, and ultimately achieve their goals.

Right around the same time that I read *Give and Take*, I had a meeting with a young entrepreneur who was working in artificial intelligence. He was brilliant and his mind was next level. As he was speaking, I could sense that he wasn't feeling okay. He told me he was on an exhausting fundraising roadshow, with meeting after meeting. I knew he had young kids and I started to wonder what it was like being away from them for long periods of time. After listening to him speak for a while, I said, "What's going on with you? Forget the business for a moment. Are you okay?"

I was surprised when he started crying. He said, "I can't believe you asked me that. I've had 50 meetings with investors, and not one of them asked about me or how I am—all they cared about was the numbers." It dawned on me that I work in a field full of takers.

Similar to earlier in my life, when I realized I was perpetuating a "takers" game by helping advertisers use psychology to make a lot of money from consumers buying their stuff, I began to see how the same game was being played in the world of venture capital. It is a game of extraction, where the underlying motive is to take value from entrepreneurs and founders, even if it costs them their MEPS well-being. I knew I was having my own moment with that kind of greed. But by that point, I was done with perpetuating the Matrix and the system.

I chose to reframe my perspective from "What can I get out of this?" to "How can I be of service?" This practice is part of letting life happen through me and being in the highest service possible. This more freeing and expansive approach allowed for me to have serendipity in connection.

One way to think about our relationships with people is to see them as constellations. We each find one another through the great mystery and form beautiful connections of light. Every interaction and relationship is an opportunity for transformation, healing, and strengthening of our sense of self. We need to see the other person as an energetic being who has manifested in front of us and ask, "What does the universe want for us?"

We all have our unique vantage points, and building strong relationships with integrity and trust can expand our awareness through those different perspectives. Our individual apertures of experience and reality can become an expansive opening through connection and love, allowing us to see, learn, and experience even more. Of course, the resonance between people is crucial. I don't believe in forcing a connection, but if there is one, it becomes an act of exploration to see how I can be of service and support the other person while living my own purpose. We each have our own purpose, and that purpose is ultimately tied to serving the people around us.

However, it's important to maintain clear boundaries and practice sovereignty, meaning we need to prioritize our own needs and well-being while also surrendering to the constellations of our relationships. Boundaries are a very important part of building resilience—they help us keep our constellations sacred and clear of unwanted energy or others' attempts to highjack our reality. People who are completely plugged into the Matrix can easily manifest in your field to disrupt your flow. Being in relationship with other people is a continual and delicate process of finding that balance between being of service to others and taking care of our mental, emotional, physical, and spiritual well-being.

KNOW YOUR VALUES

In the following exercise, you're going to get clear on your values, interests, and abilities. Values represent the qualities that are most important to you, like compassion, awareness, spirituality, and commitment to growth. Interests are the things you love to spend your time doing, like yoga, cooking, running, and writing. Abilities are the things you're good at and bring to the table, like listening, organizing events, bringing people together, and problem solving.

Think of your values, interests, and abilities as the way that you connect to other people. Most relationships struggle because of a lack of connection in one or all three of these areas, so knowing this about yourself will help you identify your points of connection with another person.

Copy the following Venn diagram onto a blank piece of paper and then fill in each circle. Feel free to use what you've discovered in the previous chapters to fill in some of your answers. Use the diagram to build your confidence in what you bring to a group and to identify where you might find people who align with you.

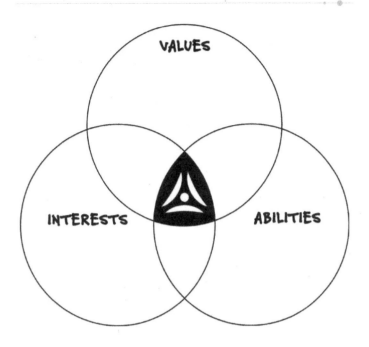

When you attract the right people, your network multiplies. Here are some of the qualities you want to look for:

- You support each other's ambition and goals.

- You provide each other with new capabilities.

- You provide each other with new resources.

- You create new opportunities for each other.

- You connect each other to new networks.

When you look at the Venn diagram you made, notice the abilities you bring to the world and what you have to offer others. Come up with a list of 10 dream people you'd like to meet who have the qualities you value. If you can't think of a specific person, come up with an idea of who they are, such as a business mentor who can help you get to the next step. Make these specific to the goals and ambitions you have for yourself.

YOUR CORE GROUP

Jim Rohn said it, and Tony Robbins and a host of others have repeated it over and over. We are the average of the five people we spend the most time with. If your friend smokes, you are 61 percent more likely to smoke.[3] This snapshot shows the direct effect people around us have on our lives, and the importance of surrounding ourselves with people who align with our values.

Too often, we get comfortable in our relationships and no longer strive to grow or challenge one another. We don't take time to reevaluate whether a relationship is serving us. Relationships are energy exchanges. The quality and balance of the exchange have a direct impact on our well-being and sense of freedom.

Do a relationship audit:

1. **Reflect on your current relationships.**
   Take some time to think about the different relationships in your life and how they make you feel. Make a list of the people you have relationships with, and consider whether they are positive, negative, or neutral.

2. **Identify areas of improvement.** Once you have a clear understanding of your relationships, identify areas where they could be improved. This could include things like communication, trust, or shared goals.

3. **Communicate with your partner or friend.** Have an open and honest conversation with

your partner or friend about the relationship. Share your thoughts and feelings, and ask for their input as well.

4. **Set goals.** Once you've identified areas of improvement, set specific, measurable goals for how you can work to improve how you show up in the relationship.

5. **Monitor progress.** Regularly check in on your progress toward your goals, and make adjustments as needed.

6. **Seek outside help.** If you find you're unable to improve a relationship on your own, consider seeking the help of a therapist or counselor.

7. **Be grateful.** Remember to express and share your gratitude to the people in your life and the positive relationships you have. Make a note about everyone you feel grateful for and share it with them. Commit to ongoing communication and growth in every relationship.

So, we've looked at how to evaluate your relationships and whether they are truly serving you.

Our relationship choices reflect the way we see ourselves. If we don't see our own value, then we choose others who don't see it either. If we don't believe our time is valuable, we choose people who don't value our time. To call in relationships that serve us, we must be clear about our values, interests, and abilities.

SEEING A NEW VIEW

A book called *On Relationship* had a huge impact on me. The author, Jiddu Krishnamurti, showed the correlations between how we handle personal crises, relationships, and the problems of the world. To solve the big problems like homelessness, war, and illiteracy, we must start by reconciling with estranged family members, keeping our homes in order, and respecting others. He said, "If we are concerned with our own lives, if we understand our relationship with others, we will have created a new society; otherwise, we will perpetuate the present chaotic mess and confusion."[4] Inevitably, every relationship will hit a point of struggle. Maybe your ideas conflict or there are hurt feelings over an event or words said. There's a framework that I like to use to help me understand the people I care about, and it's called VIEW. I learned this from one of my teachers, Joe Hudson, an executive coach who works with leaders from all over the world. It's a lens you can use to engage your awareness:

- V: Vulnerable
- I: Impartial
- E: Empathetic
- W: Wonder

If you maintain this perspective while you engage, you'll be able to truly hear others—rather than reacting to them based on your own conceptions and emotions.

Let's say you struggle to connect with someone in your family because you have different beliefs about how the world works. Maybe you feel triggered every time you talk to them about a certain topic, but you love them and want them in your life.

First, approaching the situation with vulnerability means that you're open to learning and hearing another perspective and you're open to sharing how you feel in a conscientious way.

Second, notice if you've got an agenda. Do you need to be right? Do you need to convince them? They can feel that. Drop the agenda and adopt a stance of impartiality so you can truly listen to what they have to say.

Third, connect through empathy and notice what happens. Use affirming words to let them know you're listening. Ask them to share how they feel.

Finally, engage your sense of wonder and curiosity. Get genuinely curious about what they're sharing, and use clean, clear questions that start with "what" or "how." Stay away from using loaded questions that assume an outcome, which will immediately put them on the defensive.

Remember, the conversation doesn't have to be long. You don't have to engage for hours, and you don't have to reach some kind of conclusion where you all agree. The point here isn't consensus—it's connection.

CREATING NEW CONNECTIONS

My life drastically changed when I attended my first personal development workshop. It was the first time I was in a room with other human beings who were there solely to become a better version of themselves. It's not that I resonated with every single person there. I'm not sure I keep in contact with even one person I met in that workshop. But the turning point was seeing that there actually were spaces where I was free to be my most authentic self.

From there, I committed to putting myself in as many situations with like-minded people as I possibly could. Personal and business development is expensive, especially if you want to be in the same room with a multitude of inspiring and successful people. But if you can commit to attending just one event that sparks your interest, doors will open to you that you never thought possible. Maybe one connection you make will invite you to a roundtable dinner they're hosting with other inspiring humans, or a group of you will plan a transformational weekend where each person shares a unique gift and offering.

This may sound out of reach as you're reading this, but the formula is clear. Plant yourself in spaces that excite and inspire you, and you will meet the people who will expedite your growth and opportunities.

CHAPTER 5 POWER PLAYS

❏ Print out the survival plan, food guide, and survival kit checklists.

❏ Go through the survival plan checklist:
1. Check off what you already have in place.
2. In yellow, highlight the items you don't have that feel easy to start with.
3. In pink, highlight the items that feel more challenging to put in place, and without rushing, set times to take action on them over the coming weeks.
4. Make a list of whom you can enroll to help you.

- [ ] Put together/order your emergency food supply based on your family's needs. Start with a food supply for three days to one week, and then gradually increase.

- [ ] Put together/order a survival kit.

- [ ] Do a relationship audit using the seven steps outlined here.

- [ ] Complete your Values, Interests, and Abilities Venn diagram.

- [ ] Come up with a list of 10 dream people you would like to meet who have the qualities you listed in your diagram.

- [ ] Take action from your relationship audit to ensure you limit time with people who don't support your growth and spend more time with people who do.

6

THE WEALTHY SPIRITUAL WARRIOR

I wish people could realize all their dreams and wealth and fame so that they could see it is not where you are going to find your sense of completion.

— JIM CARREY

We've usually seen the words *wealthy* and *spiritual* placed in opposition. The same goes for *spiritual* and *warrior*. This Key is where we integrate all of these ideas.

As a New Millionaire, you have already redefined wealth. It's about *impact* rather than money. The next steps are to understand *spiritual* and *warrior* in relationship to your soul and feel how these qualities flow seamlessly into a practical approach for how you live, work, and play.

When it all comes together, you will see there is nothing paradoxical about becoming a wealthy spiritual warrior.

SOUL AND SPIRIT

Soul and spirit are often used interchangeably, but they represent different aspects of our being.

The soul is a drop in the ocean. It is the individual expression of our unique identity within the universal consciousness. The soul is the seat of our emotions, our desires, and our personality. It is what makes us who we are as individuals. Our *soul* is our essence, the immaterial part of ourselves that is ever-changing yet everlasting.

The spirit, on the other hand, is the ocean itself. It is the universal consciousness, the source of all creation. It is the infinite and formless essence that underlies all of existence and the unchanging and eternal aspect of our being. It gives us a sense of oneness with all of creation. Spirit is the vitality and energy of the soul, its heartbeat and reflection. It is the current through which our soul communicates with the fabric of the entire universe as well as our human body.

The more connected we are to our soul, the higher our spiritual well-being will be. You may feel sadness when you're not listening to your soul. The source of emotional pain is disconnection from the soul.

It's okay if that all seems a bit ethereal. In this Key, we're going to move to a higher plane *and* bring concepts down to earth. In doing so, we'll dive deep and take practical steps. I invite you to enjoy the dance.

When you're connected to your soul, you can access its infinite energy and potential, which is spirit (and has movement or inertia). To be spiritual is to have an open channel to this source of infinite energy and possibilities.

Spiritual well-being can be measured by the level of quality and depth of your connection with your soul.

Sadly, our souls too often get overlooked. That's why when people come to me for guidance, I ask, "What does your soul want?" I find asking that question opens people up. It's a potent opportunity to demystify their soul and regain connection. Their answers vary. Some will say, "My soul wants to scream," or, "My soul wants to run around naked in a field of daisies and cry." Others will say, "My soul wants to be understood, to be seen and heard." And sometimes, more often than you may think, I receive a mystified look followed by silence.

I was working with an uber-logical executive who was so regimented that just about every minute of his life was scheduled. I asked him, "What does your soul want?" He didn't know what to say, which by no means did I interpret as him not knowing what his soul wanted. I simply felt he had lost the connection with his soul. This led me to ask, "How do you communicate with your soul?"

After getting another blank stare, I asked, "Does your soul have to schedule time with your assistant? Does it require a calendar invite?"

He smiled, as did I. It was by design, since nothing blocks connection with our soul like a dysregulated nervous system, and smiling helps regulate our emotions. The metaphor of the assistant was spot-on, since our souls do have gatekeepers. These gatekeepers are our own defense mechanisms that we have unconsciously created in order to avoid feeling our emotions. Sometimes what we think we want is different from what our soul truly wants, because of the programming from the Matrix. Getting in touch with this part of ourselves can be challenging. This is why we have to build practices to *re*connect us with our souls and build a better relationship with them.

When you nurture this connection, your life opens up to miracles. It's not a quick fix, but over time and with a little effort (actually, *less* effort!) and patience, your soul will begin to come online. It will help remind you of your place in the world and why you are here. Nurturing your soul will change the way you perceive the world.

Here are some of the signs you can expect when your soul is coming online:

15 Signs That Your Soul Is Coming Online

1. More coincidences and serendipities in your life (read the book *The Alchemist*)

2. A deeper connection to your own intuition

3. A sense of calm and peace in your mind

4. Spontaneous smiles and feelings of gratitude

5. Feeling connected to nature and the cosmos

6. Feelings of love replacing feelings of fear

7. Life decisions becoming easy and seamless

8. You have a mission instead of a business

9. Abundance flows

10. Feelings of generosity and giving to others

11. Being in service to the collective

12. You notice you judge others less and have more compassion

13. Your heart feels open

14. Having amazing results in life and business but not being attached to them

15. A feeling of oneness and interconnectedness

THE TRUTH IS MULTIDIMENSIONAL

Connecting with your soul creates an expanded awareness of experience. Rather than reacting to your emotions, you start to feel them and allow them to move through you. In doing so, you stop resisting what's happening and start to see that two things can be true at the same time. I've been frustrated at a client *and* immensely grateful for his business. I've been at wit's end with my kids *and* in deep appreciation of what they're teaching me. I've fought fervently for environmental protection *and* acknowledged the propaganda that accompanies it.

This perspective frees up what really needs to come through. Instead of either-or, it's both. Inflation is nerve-wracking, *and* you're grateful to live in a world of abundance where you can afford nourishing food.

Improv actors are taught to reflexively say, "Yes *and* . . ." just as spiritual warriors learn to say, "Both *and* . . ." The glass is *both* half full *and* half empty, *and* I don't even know if it's a glass, *and* I'm so happy to have water, *and* I'm worried about the chemicals in the water. Binary choices are limiting, create conflict, and reduce creativity.

When you connect with your soul, you start to see that *all* things can be true at once. In fact, Einstein said, "It seems as though we must use sometimes the one theory and sometimes the other, while at times we may use either. We are faced with a new kind of difficulty. We have two contradictory pictures of reality; separately neither of them fully explains the phenomena of light, but together they do."[1]

The idea that two things can be true at once has all sorts of ramifications. It encourages understanding and softens conflict. It also allows us to acknowledge the wide range of emotions that we are constantly feeling.

In this moment, we can celebrate where we are now *and* get excited about the even more abundant rewards to come. On our journey of consciousness, we seek to have roots *and* wings, to stabilize *and* soar. In fact, the whole point of building a foundation is so we can transcend the material plane. You are now starting to see that this is *not* a paradox; this is the beautiful dance where all things can be true at once.

You can see the parallels between our journey and Maslow's Hierarchy of Needs. The gist is to move from the bottom of the pyramid to the top by solidifying yourself before reaching higher levels of consciousness.

The lower rungs on the hierarchy focus on safety, security, and stability. At the top of Maslow's hierarchy, as most of us know it, is "self-actualization." It actually goes even higher. My friend Nichol Bradford pointed out, "Later in his life, after the hierarchy had been published, Maslow began work on a final stage of human motivation.

SELF-ACTUALIZATION
Desire to become the most that one can be

ESTEEM
Respect, Self-Esteem, Status, Recognition, Strength, Freedom

LOVE & BELONGING
Friendship, Intimacy, Family, Sense of Connection

SAFETY NEEDS
Personal Security, Employment, Resources, Health, Property

PHYSIOLOGICAL NEEDS
Air, Water, Food, Shelter, Sleep, Clothing, Reproduction

Self-actualization was not the pinnacle of individual human achievement, but rather self-transcendence. Not an elevation of the self, but a subverting of it."[2]

Here we are, ready to explore higher levels of consciousness and then ascend to self-transcendence. You are ready to take this journey and go beyond the three-dimensional world, because you have solidified your MEPS well-being. Ideally, your journey takes you from *profit* to *prophet*—you recognize that you are here to deliver a higher truth from your higher self that operates multidimensionally.

When you connect with your soul, you are able to access a higher intelligence that resides outside of the Matrix, and you are then able to channel that wisdom and higher intelligence back into the Matrix on demand. In doing so, you can use your superpowers to set up your own game in multiple dimensions.

MEET YOUR INNER WARRIOR

Now that we have explored what *wealthy* and *spiritual* mean, let's define *warrior*. What I love about this definition is how it reinforces that two things can be true at once:

1. (especially in former times) a brave or experienced soldier or fighter: "the warrior heroes of ancient Greece";

2. any of a number of standing poses in yoga in which the legs are held apart and the arms are stretched outward.[3]

Put them together, and the warrior is a brave soul who *takes a stand*. It doesn't necessarily mean he or she goes into combat. A warrior serves humanity. A warrior fights to discover his or her purpose and stay on that path.

Warriors have typically been seen as men, but the new paradigm needs women who also can come back to their inner power. If you're a woman reading this and feel as though you can't be a warrior, ask yourself where this belief may have come from. If you're a man reading this and your only vision of warriors is men, ask how that vision impacts your perception and how it may be limiting you. All it takes is being present for a childbirth to see how women are the ultimate warriors. Men can learn from women what it truly means to take a stand and serve humanity. Women are often the best teachers for how to balance a gentle heart with a fighting spirit.

The warrior is a brave soul who *takes a stand.*

We all know what it's like to feel passionate about something that matters to us—there's an innate part of us that wants to take a stand and fight for the things we believe in. It's why we start nonprofits, build families, scale businesses, compete in triathlons, join movements, and cheer for the underdog.

Whether we go by the name of Scythians, Spartans, or samurais, across cultures, we are all warriors. Each one of us battles every day to define and defend our sense of purpose, to justify our existence on this planet, and to understand, if only within our own hearts and minds, who we are and what we believe in.

Take a moment to think about being a spiritual warrior and what it means to you. Ask yourself:

- Is the fight internal or external, or is it both? Is it a fight, or is it a dance?

- Do we fight by a code? If so, what is it?

- What is the warrior archetype? Where did it come from? What form does it take today?

- How can we use the archetype to elevate and awaken our species?

Warriors are not only persons in armor, but teachers, artists, entrepreneurs, and all other walks of life can be warriors too.

RIVALRIES DIMINISH OUR TRUE WARRIOR ENERGY

When not expressed, the need to take a stand for something turns into an either-or. In modern society, this takes the form of choosing sides in celebrity gossip, political extremism, road rage, meaningless debates with friends or family, and becoming fanatical sports fans.

A key strategy of the Matrix is to divide and conquer. The term *divide and conquer,* from the Latin phrase *divide et impera,* is as old as politics and war. The strategy to divide your enemy so you can reign is attributed to Julius Caesar, who successfully applied it to conquering Gaul 22 centuries ago.

Sports, politics, and entertainment understand how this formula works. One of the main tenets of storytelling is that there must be a protagonist and an antagonist, a hero and a villain. It's how Big Entertainment mines our attention so we open our wallets. Grabbing people's attention by pitting two sides against each other works for ratings, and on a broader scale, it continues to work to "divide et impera." It keeps most people stuck in the Matrix, criticizing the other political party and making enemies with those who don't agree with their binary choice. Apropos to just how pervasive the "divide and conquer" strategy is, one of the leading daily fantasy sports companies is named FanDuel. All the rage and righteousness keep us distracted so we keep arguing, working, and consuming.

Though nuanced issues deserve nuanced dialogue, the Matrix knows better. I can tell you from experience that no one clicks on the headline, "The Pros and Cons of Higher Education," yet "5 Reasons Why College Is a Rip-Off" maximizes the click-through rate. The choices in the Matrix are binary: pro-life or pro-choice; masks or no masks; Republican or Democrat.

Even in lighter conversations about pop culture, people love to compare greatness. Who is the greatest of all time (GOAT): Jordan or LeBron? Biggie or Tupac? Prince or Michael Jackson? That question, in particular, gives me tingles given my love for MJ. But why must my love for the King of Pop be coupled with comparing him to Prince? And who needed to label such greatness as the "king" of anything?

The most anticipated moments in sports, in fact, are *rivalries.* In hockey, team rivalries like the Boston Bruins vs. the Montreal Canadiens and individual rivalries like Sidney Crosby vs. Alex Ovechkin inspire emotion. The website TheSportster noted, "Perhaps the National Hockey League came into existence for one thing: To create blood, sweat, tears and heated rivalries. In all honesty, there is nothing more entertaining in professional sports."[4]

I may not have been aware of this as a kid, but I sure loved to watch hockey. Like many Canadian kids, I worshipped Wayne Gretzky. When I was seven and he was traded from the Edmonton Oilers to the Los Angeles Kings, it felt like *I* was being abandoned in favor of the glitz and glamor of Hollywood. I continued to play hockey and watch it religiously. Others may have labeled my obsession as an escape from reality, but it was actually a welcome escape from my home life.

What I didn't understand then was how watching hockey kept me from expressing my warrior spirit in ways that were aligned with my soul. Only after a pastime turned into an obsession did I learn the hard way. As I share my story, you'll see how you can channel your warrior energy in such a way that it aligns with your soul.

HOW THE MATRIX STOLE $601.7 MILLION FROM ME

How and why did hockey become so important for me? From childhood, I noticed that most conversations between adult men centered around sports and arguing about which players or teams are better. This practice has been passed on from generation to generation.

This is super relevant today with so many groups getting together for fantasy football drafts, Super Bowl parties, and fight nights. There are now even massive e-sports battles—people fill stadiums to watch two teams contend in a video game for huge cash prizes. The fact that gamers are getting recognized for their talent is great. But what concerns me is how the spectator element has consumed too much of our warrior energy, leaving less space for our soul's expression.

I would be taking a page from the Matrix by saying these things are "bad" when, in fact, they are complex. Let's remember that all things can be true at once. We have to ask ourselves: How else are we expressing our warrior energy? And what does it cost us when we devote so much time to voyeuristic events?

When I was 20, I did what any fine young man with a few Canadian dollars in his pocket would do: I bought season tickets to the Vancouver Canucks. I would put on my Pavel Bure jersey, get the pregame party started over cocktails with my friends, and then root for *my* team from the stands.

I did this for 10 years, continuing to upgrade my seats and VIP passes. But when I met Sukhi, I started to sell some of my tickets. That made my obsession more of a win-win. The nights I sold the tickets, I still enjoyed watching the team on TV, especially since I had made money on the deal. As a ticket seller, I was also more in tune with group psychology, watching demand for seats ebb and flow based on how the team was doing. When the Canucks sucked, it was easy to get tickets. When they were good, everyone jumped on the bandwagon.

In 2011, the Canucks made it to the Stanley Cup finals—the Super Bowl of hockey. By then, I was a husband, so I didn't go to nearly as many games, but I certainly wasn't going to miss the chance to watch *my* team win a championship.

When the Canucks won game five in the best of seven to take a 3–2 series lead against the Boston Bruins, I couldn't help but think about what it would be like to celebrate in Boston when the Canucks clinched the Cup. This brought up the question: How much did it cost to buy tickets and fly to Boston on short notice?

Those who know me have heard me respond to doubt or disbelief in any number of unrealistic situations with a simple, "Everything is possible." I wasn't going to let money stand in the way of making some magic happen, and you'd better believe I was in the mood for magic when it came to the Stanley Cup finals.

As I look back on the day before game six in Boston, I see three screens in front of me. One screen had my business dashboard with all the daily metrics of our online traffic platform where I could turn the dial to increase click-through rate. The other had StubHub showing ticket prices. The third displayed Mt. Gox, where I tracked Bitcoin and was contemplating buying some. I chose not to buy Bitcoin in favor of buying tickets to the Stanley Cup.

While I can see the absurdity of my convictions now, back then there was no amount I wasn't willing to spend on both hockey and airline tickets. Boston hadn't won a Stanley Cup in 39 years, so tickets were hotter than my mom's tikka masala. I spent a fortune, which in retrospect wasn't even my dumbest decision. That honor went to my choice to wear my number 10 Pavel Bure jersey to a Boston bar before the game and then keep it on *during* the game. It's a miracle I didn't get my ass kicked.

That's not to say I made a *bad* decision by choosing hockey over bitcoin. Spending money on experiences or any type of play has its place. But in this case, it came from a place of ego and lack of a connection with my soul.

HIJACKING OUR WARRIOR EXPRESSION IS AS OLD AS TIME

Boston showed me sports fandom at another level. It was mob mentality at its finest, and even as focused as I was on hockey at this point, the intensity of the Boston fans made me think that something wasn't right. The energy I felt was ugly. It seemed to me like everyone felt they had permission to bully anyone who wasn't cheering for their team. I spoke to one man who said that a Boston fan peed on him because he was wearing his Canucks jersey. Luckily I was a with a group of people, but this man was alone and suffered for it. I can laugh about it now, but at the time it felt like unbridled aggression. It really made me question what I was doing in that kind of environment.

A massive part of human culture is obsessed with sports. The collective consciousness longs to see battle and get a taste of being a warrior. This goes back to the

Romans, where gladiators fought in the Colosseum as spectators nearly rioted. All the while, politicians choreographed mass psychosis with grins on their faces as they designed the feudal system and counted their loot.

I, too, was channeling my warrior spirit in the wrong direction. I fell hook, line, and sinker for the divide-and-conquer machinations of the Matrix and happily turned over my money and attention.

My beloved Canucks weren't doing much better. *We* got our butts kicked, 5–2. If the game itself wasn't bad enough, after every goal, I had dozens of rowdy Bostonians screaming at me, "Hey, Canuck, you suck! How you like them apples?" I haven't been able to watch *Good Will Hunting* since.

I flew back to Vancouver and had a choice to make: sell my game-seven tickets and recoup what I had spent in Boston, or go to the deciding game and subject myself to unrequited love? Days earlier, we had learned that Sukhi was pregnant, which made my decision even harder.

So what did I do, after fielding ridiculous offers to sell my tickets?

I went to the game.

You can't judge me any more harshly than I later judged myself. Once the game started, I could only hold on to false hope for so long. There was no drama; just a 4–0 ass-whooping by the Bruins, which is exactly how it felt to me.

A CITY AND A SOUL IN RUIN

When the final second ticked off the clock, I had an out-of-body experience. I was no longer a Canucks fan watching the game, but a soul watching the game. I saw generations of patriarchal fandom and aggression channeled through sports fanatics who excused their animal-like behavior with "city pride."

I heard the public address announcer, who no longer sounded like Josh Ashbridge but the voice of the Matrix, plugging me more deeply into the system. It felt like my head was going to explode, and it wasn't from the loss we had just endured. It was from the realization that I had been taken advantage of, and there was only one person to turn a finger back at: myself. When I snapped back to reality, a question filled with shame raced through my mind: What the fuck had I spent all that time, attention, money, and energy on?

My hockey fandom had returned nothing of value. I'd bought into the narrative that my sports team was part of my identity. I had done exactly as the league owners, TV executives, liquor companies, and apparel makers had told me to do. I'd bought everything they'd sold. I'd given my dollars, my time, and my heart—and, even worse, my soul—to something that could never love me back.

Just as I was judging those Boston Massholes for their vigilantism, my Vancouverites one-upped them. According to reports, a group was heard chanting, "Let's go riot, let's go riot" during the first period of the game. They hadn't even cared who won. They'd used the situation as an excuse to pour their warrior energy into something, just as I had poured mine into cheering for the team. These misguided warriors started with flipping cars, and when that got old, moved on to porta potties with people in them. The city stank as bad as the hockey team that night. Four people were stabbed, nine police officers were injured, and 101 people were arrested.[5,6]

As I mourned the loss of my team and the destruction of my city, I realized that the main source of my frustration was myself. I, the attention miner, got mined. I, the wizard of psychology, got duped. I, the puppet master of incentivizing behavior, became the puppet.

In business-speak, I had incurred massive opportunity costs. I had invested 10 years of my life into a venture that yielded negative returns. To be even more precise, let's say I took what I spent on the 2011 playoffs alone (including tickets, merch, and travel to Boston), which was U.S. $20,000, and bought bitcoin (BTC) on the day the Stanley Cup playoffs began. On April 13, 2011, one BTC was worth U.S. $0.92, which would have allowed me to buy 21,739 BTC. As of April 24, 2023, its value was U.S. $27,680.50, which equates to $601,746,390. That's 601.7 *million* U.S. dollars, my friends, just to watch a bunch of grown-up boys knocking around a hockey puck.

No wonder I was becoming spiritually bankrupt.

Once I got past the shame, I started asking more practical questions: If I had put that fanatical emotion and money into something else, what could I have done? This one simple question broke the spell and ushered me onto a new path forward.

Many of us have been raised to pay attention to the external voices from our parents, teachers, and media, all the while ignoring our soul's wisdom. Because of this, we have become disconnected from who we truly are and the messages that are ours to receive. Every human being has the ability to access his or her soul, yet few ever do.

We're designed to be hunters and gatherers, and our prey is now mostly confined to the basin of the Amazon— the online superstore, that is. Think about Edward Norton's character in the film *Fight Club*. He said that we are no longer hunter-gatherers, we are consumers. When Norton's character saw that he was stuck in the Matrix, he used fighting as an outlet for his warrior nature. Turning to a punching bag made him feel alive because, after a fight, the volume on everything else in his life got turned down.

The same goes for figures in sports, politics, and entertainment. They turn the volume up so we can disconnect from our thoughts. They allow us to zone out so we can block out the calling from our souls.

That's why I made the decision to get out. I gave up my season tickets and burned my Pavel Bure jersey. Fine, okay, I didn't really burn it; I sold it on eBay. And it's a good thing I did, because my first son was born shortly after and I was only at the beginning of my journey to explore consciousness. In a way, it was easy for me to divert my spiritual warrior energy to my new family. My son made me ask questions like "What do I want to model?" and "Where do I want my energy to go?" My mission in life became clearer, and I understood the work that I was doing in a new way and made the conscious decision to pour my energy into something worthwhile, to build a world I wanted my son to live in.

This is not to say that I was *only* watching hockey for the previous decade. I was still exploring consciousness then, but most of my work was outwardly directed. I was pointing fingers. I was asking lots of questions, but mostly of others, and I had failed to understand how my internal world was creating my external world.

THE INTERNAL WORLD CREATES THE EXTERNAL WORLD

Let's double-click on that. *My internal world was creating my external world.* This moment in my life was like an M. Night Shyamalan movie, where everything that made no sense suddenly came together in harmony. Up until that point, I believed that the world was a dark place, but this experience illuminated the fact that the world is just a reflection of our collective unconsciousness—and my unconsciousness. It manifests as the yin and the yang of the external world I see around me. In other words, I am the co-creator of the Matrix.

My internal world was creating my external world.

You co-create your reality based on your state of consciousness. The bidirectional feedback loop that we have with the Matrix gets displayed through our reality distortion field (RDF), where our thoughts co-produce the contents on the screen. In other words, our thoughts *create* our reality, and our internal world *becomes* our external world. If our internal world is unconscious, then that unconsciousness contributes to our reality. If you are operating from a lower state of consciousness, then your interplay with the Matrix works so that its inputs (media, education, parents, and others that we discussed in Key 1) have more power over you and take over your RDF. However, when you connect to your soul and realize the truth of your essence, then you operate from a higher state of consciousness and are able to shape-shift with the system, in a way, to establish your own RDF. As a result, the Matrix begins to work for you rather than against you.

Once I started to see that the external is a reflection of the internal, my next step was to turn inward and start asking questions such as: *Who am I? What is my purpose? What is the nature of consciousness?* The best way to work on our internal world is through awareness. Continue to ask that powerful question: Am I thinking my own thoughts? When you notice a trigger from the outside world, watch where your thoughts and emotions go. When you feel you're not at a place of equanimity, that's a sign that your internal world needs attention. Ignore it and react to the external, and you will likely make unconscious decisions.

On a collective level, when we don't heal the internal, that unconsciousness becomes the Matrix. This also means that on a collective level, when we raise our consciousness, we can take a revolutionary leap in our species and live in an external world that reflects our inner harmony.

The chains that bind us are only our own. We've taken this journey to see that we, ourselves, have co-created a Matrix. And by embracing consciousness, we now get to choose how we continue to co-create it, when we want to step out of it, and how we can create a new reality that is reflected in the external world.

Instead of seeing people and events in the world around me as a source of aversion, something to avoid, I started to see that I could experience the nature of reality through every single one of my experiences, whether I labeled them "good" or "bad." It was no longer something that happened to me; I created it. Even hobbies like hockey changed from an unconscious choice to a conscious one. In *The Matrix*, you might remember that moment in the movie when Cypher sold everyone out because he just wanted to eat a steak and have his wine. It's kinda like that, only you don't need to sell anyone out—you can still be in it and enjoy it, just be aware of what you're doing.

In that reality, you will find the full expression of your warriorship. The desire to be a warrior, to stand for something and fight for something, continues to live inside our souls. To achieve spiritual sovereignty, we have to learn how to channel the wisdom that lives inside of us. We'll return to this in a moment after you see the surprising way hockey came back into my life.

A RETURN TO THE MATRIX . . . WITH A TWIST

This is where things get fun! The moment you understand the Matrix and step out of it is the moment you are free to jump back in and enjoy all the wonders it has to offer. When I was in Orlando with Sukhi last year and we heard that LeBron James and the Lakers were in town to play the Magic, we bought tickets. Just like seeing a great work of art, we enjoyed celebrating the greatness of this extraordinary human.

Because we've been able to unplug from the Matrix, we can plug back in on demand. This is why we now love the Matrix. Instead of fighting it, we see it for what it is and decide when and how we want to play both inside and outside of it. You can live in it knowingly and fight for your own truth, rather than follow what others are programming you to do.

We go to the movies and take our kids with us. When we want a quiet dinner, we'll put on a movie for the three boys. Of course, we make a thoughtful choice, but we also allow them to play inside the Matrix. With awareness, it's simply a different way to engage with the three-dimensional world.

Since the universe loves to give us what we need, it gifted me a son who loves hockey. Do I refuse to let him watch games and lecture him on how I love him too much to let him make the same mistakes that I made? That, my friends, would be unconscious AF! Besides, at age 11, Jaxon is too smart for that and can see past my BS. With healthy boundaries and communication, we can set up structures that support the highest good. This explains why I often watch games with him, and we not only talk about hockey, but also the commercials and how they fit into the bigger picture. I have the best time artfully playing inside the Matrix.

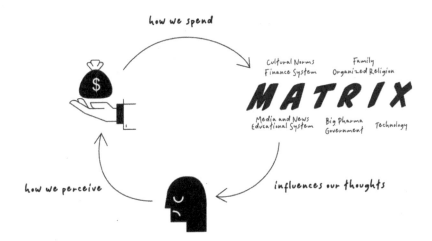

This is a big distinction, because before, we were saying the Matrix is "bad" and controlling you. Now that we understand that the external is the internal, we open up the concept that the "bad" is only a reflection of our consciousness. It makes the expression "be the change you want to see in the world" ring true.

You can play all you want in the realms of sports, entertainment, and politics. The key is to recognize when your thoughts have been hijacked. Draw from that state of consciousness, and channel it to become fanatical about something connected to your soul, not your ego. A warrior serves humanity while also cultivating his or her own spirituality.

I'M STARTING WITH THE MAN IN THE MIRROR

Once we've realized that our inner is the outer and our outer is the inner, we see how it's incumbent upon us to harness our warrior power. Our outer reality is created by our inner reality, which is why if we want to change our outer world, we have to change our inner. Each one of us is made up of a lifetime (and beyond) of experiences, memories, and traumas. Whether we are aware of it or not, the world and reality we see is directly correlated to what is stored in our body.

We must focus on healing our inner landscape and the traumas that are stored inside, so we can create the reality we want to see. There are many ways to begin to explore our inner landscape in a healthy and supported way; it's important to find a support system that you can lean on through this journey. Oftentimes the people directly around us cannot relate to or understand the shifts we are going through, so it may take looking outside your immediate circle for support.

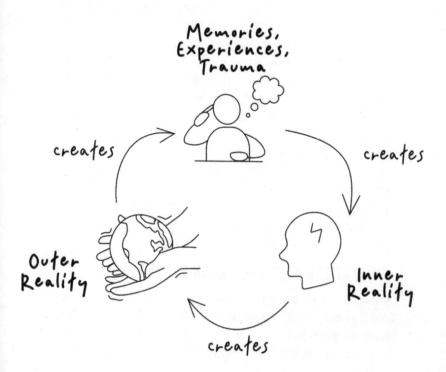

THE WEALTHY SPIRITUAL WARRIOR

Our overall goal is to become a *wealthy spiritual warrior*. Wealth is *health*, in the broadest definition of the word. It's feeling good in our bodies and in our souls. It's healthy relationships with others and a healthy relationship with abundance.

In Key 3, we used a dictionary definition of *spirituality*: "the quality of being concerned with the human spirit or soul as opposed to material or physical things." But it goes much deeper than that. It's about understanding that there is more than meets the eye: the interconnectedness of all things. Just like gravity isn't something you can see, whether or not you acknowledge it, it's always present. Gravity, like spirituality, is a powerful force of the universe that governs our every moment. To be a "spiritual person" is to be one who is living from his or her heart, trusting the universe, aligned with the soul, and expanding consciousness.

A warrior is one *who takes a stand* and serves humanity. A warrior fights to discover his or her purpose and stay on that path. A warrior appreciates his or her gifts, sees trauma and adversity as teachers, finds a way to forgive, and takes those lessons to give back and fight to raise consciousness. When we put it all together, we arrive here:

A **wealthy spiritual warrior** is of sound health, connected to spirit, and takes a stand for his or her purpose. He or she knows the tricks of the Matrix and stands firm in the commitment to freedom, purpose, and abundance. In doing so, the warrior cultivates connection to the soul and channels that infinite wisdom to create a positive impact on the world.

Letting go of my hockey tickets was part of the shift that allowed me to direct my energy toward my purpose—focusing on impact rather than profit. I began to take a stand for my ideas, for my business partners, and for consciousness. This was the beginning of my quest to become a New Millionaire.

As a result, all areas of my MEPS well-being improved while I earned plenty of money to support and nurture my growing family. It looked like this:

Mental

Instead of thinking about games, I started diving deeper into cryptocurrency and solving problems through consciousness.

Emotional

I had so much more bandwidth to be patient and loving with my family. It made the birth of my son a joyous time and, without the distraction of hockey, I was even more present.

Physical

All that kinetic energy I had been using to cheer on the Canucks got channeled into more physical workouts and exercise and, when Jaxon was born in January 2012, into walks while pushing his stroller.

Spiritual

This is where I saw the greatest impact. All the energy I had devoted to outward things got redirected to my spirit. I continued to study consciousness and make decisions less from my ego and more from my soul.

The most important connection we can cultivate is the one with ourselves. From there, we can tap into our soul's gifts and share them with the world. The more connected we are to ourselves, the freer we are. This allows us to take a stand for what we choose and prevent outside influences from interfering with our soul's purpose. Then we can put our time, talent, and treasure toward expanding our consciousness.

CHAPTER 6 POWER PLAYS

❏ Make a list of at least five polarizing rivalries or other situations you're aware of being perpetuated in the media currently, or have been in your lifetime (e.g., Boston Bruins vs. Montreal Canadiens, pro-life vs. pro-choice).
  1. Notice which side you've "stood on" and the reasons why you've defended that side.
  2. Observe what it would feel like to look at the situation with neutrality, offering understanding and compassion to both sides.

❏ Find ways to play inside the Matrix. What activities have you labeled guilty pleasures? Ask what it would feel like if you could be 100 percent present for those activities without any self-judgment.

❏ Gain clarity about your own definition of *warrior*. Consider what you've been fighting for, how that impacts your identity, and what your soul is really telling you to fight for. Write down one to three things you stand for as a warrior.

❏ Notice the connection between your internal and external world.

1. Write down three people, words, or situations that trigger you.
2. For each one, ask yourself, "What is this telling me about my internal world?"
3. Then ask yourself, "How can I shift my internal world to transform my external world?"

7

MAGIC: THE SECRET PATHWAY TO UNLOCK UNLIMITED POSSIBILITIES

We must always be on the lookout for the presence of wonder.

— E. B. WHITE

As a kid, I loved magic. My curiosity led me to learn magic tricks and perform for friends and family. What I started noticing was that when I knew how the magic was done, I was no longer amazed or impressed by it. It actually felt like a letdown to see that it was just a sleight of hand, a special deck of cards, or an engineered contraption to create a specific illusion. What I realized was that the power of magic was not in how the trick itself was done, but the simple act of suspending all thoughts and being in the space of wonder and awe. The power is in the moments of joy, surprise, delight, and expansiveness that are felt by both the magician and the audience.

Everything we have discussed throughout this journey has been priming you to be the magician of your own life. To see beyond the veil and experience life as happening *as* you, rather than *to* you. To master your own thoughts and feel connected to your purpose and power. To foster relationships that support the desires you have, bringing in more joy and appreciation for life.

Experience life as happening *as* you, rather than *to* you.

As I'm sure you've picked up from the first six Keys, *expanding your consciousness is an inside job.* By taking responsibility to think your own thoughts and build resilience, you are now equipped to unlock the portals of magic. Because you are aligned with your most authentic self, you can now open the doors to even deeper and juicier experiences.

An expanded state of consciousness is the real magic. It's where all possibilities exist and from where we can create our desired reality. The trick itself is like seeing the sun rise. The sun itself is not the magic, but rather the cosmic orchestration that gives us light every day, plus our awe and wonder of the great mystery is the real magic. When you live from this state of being, you become an active participant in the divine unfolding of the universe itself. You become the creator and the created. You're able to use the power of your thoughts and the frequency of your energy to generate reality from the depths of your soul.

What if you could have access to this state on tap?

In this Key, I'm going to introduce to you a powerful framework that I have developed so you can easily integrate *magic* into your everyday life. I know life can get so busy that it's challenging to find time to meditate every day. This is precisely why I've optimized this process to be as efficient and effective as possible. I've refined it so that it's fast, easy, fun, and can be implemented in seven minutes per day. Would you invest seven minutes of your day to alter the lens through which you perceive and create reality?

If you notice some resistance to believing that you can invoke magic in only seven minutes each day, do a little digging to see where those thoughts come from. Are they even your own? Are you open to the possibility that you can manifest what you want through ease rather than struggle? Becoming a *New Millionaire* does not have to be difficult. As a matter of fact, the only way it works is if it is easy.

EXPERIENCING MAGIC MADE ME A BELIEVER

This Key is all about making what is seemingly impossible, *possible*. "Everything is possible" is a mantra I've brought into every area of my life, and I see believing it as the foundation of expanding consciousness. When we get out of our own way, we experience an entire world of possibility.

We see ourselves beyond the ego and get into the heart of who we are.

Some things just can't be explained in words. The best way for me to express this is to share a story that solidified my belief in magic and changed my lens for seeing the world.

It began during a family trip to Spain. Sukhi and I have always felt that raising kids as global citizens with worldly experiences would be a great way for them to grow, while also giving our family a sense of adventure. Being a New Millionaire means having the freedom to mix work, play, and discovery. I flew out a few days early for business meetings. Then I had the opportunity to take part in a meditation ceremony led by a highly skilled and trusted facilitator using a powerful entheogen (5-meo DMT) known as "the God molecule." (An entheogen is a psychoactive substance, usually from a plant, that induces alterations in perception, mood, consciousness, cognition, or behavior for the purposes of engendering spiritual development in sacred contexts.)

If you've explored the world of psychedelic medicine, you may have experienced some of the feelings and states I'm describing. If not, no worries, since it's only the beginning of the story.

For me, sitting with the God molecule was one of the most profound experiences I've ever had. I felt a lot of resistance at first, but as I surrendered and let go, I felt myself explode as if I was the Big Bang itself. I experienced myself as the universe and tasted infinity. I traversed multiple dimensions of space and time and saw the interconnectedness of all.

There was a moment where I saw a new branch of creation during a time when the collective consciousness needed it, and it showed me that my ancestry and lineage were an important piece of the puzzle for me to connect with and learn from. I saw how and why the ancient wisdom tradition of Sikhism was founded by Guru Nanak and that I was blessed with a sacred duty to channel that wisdom and reconnect to it. The medicine told me that I was a part of a revolutionary consciousness to bring about a new Earth. I am not a religious person, but for the first time in my life, I felt connected to the teachings of Sikh wisdom and nudged to look for clues there.

The next day, we went on a road trip to a beach town. I was still pretty raw and felt like I was in between dimensions. As we were driving, a store on the left side of the road caught my eye. It had a Sikh symbol (the *Khanda*) and was called Rai Supermarket. For some reason, I knew I had to stop and go in there. I told Sukhi, and she looked at me and said, "Well, go then. We will wait here in the car."

I went inside, and there was *kirtan* (traditional Sikh music in Sanskrit) playing on the speaker that immediately relaxed my nervous system. The woman in the shop was an elder who had the energy of an angel. She was radiating love and light.

I walked around to see if there were any clues for me there, and nothing really stood out besides this woman's loving energy. It was as if she had known me for lifetimes. I bought a couple beach toys for the kids and began to walk out of the store, thinking I was just making stuff up in my mind and that there was nothing there for me. As I walked out, the motherly woman slowly followed behind me. Sensing her presence, I turned around and asked, "Do you have a message for me?"

Her head tilted, her eyes softened even more, and she grinned. "Yes, son, I do. Never forget where you came from, trust the universe, and follow your heart."

I took a deep breath and did my best to let the message sink in. *Hmm . . . interesting.* Those were some nice words, and they felt warm and fuzzy, but I still didn't really feel like I got the big aha I was looking for. Even so, I trusted that the experience was exactly what it needed to be. I got back to the car, and we went on our way.

Remember that creating magic isn't a linear process and that expecting it or asking for it is the fastest way to make sure it doesn't appear.

So how do you create magic?

Keep living your life and keep the portals open. Walk around with a sense of awe and wonder. Allow, but don't force.

Jack Kornfield wrote a book wonderfully titled *After the Ecstasy, the Laundry*, which summed up my life after this profound experience. Because my perception had changed, the world looked different, though my activities were still the same—days filled with meetings, e-mails, deadlines, kids' activities, and so on.

I do believe that although your spiritual work isn't linear, it is *cumulative*. Everything you do makes an impact on your soul. When and how it manifests is the great unknown. So while I can't connect all the dots (neither do I want to), I can't separate my experience in Spain from my declaration that I would devote all my resources and energy to furthering a Conscious Thought Revolution.

Your spiritual work isn't linear, it's *cumulative.*

Soon after, I was invited to a think tank led by futurist Peter Diamandis called Abundance 360. In the midst of conversations with industry leaders, I locked eyes with a man whom I knew I was meant to meet. Harpreet is a Sikh man who was there to talk about his new company called Oura (the smart ring wearable).

His story was amazingly similar to mine. He had been playing the Old Millionaire's game, managing a multi-billion-dollar hedge fund and climbing the Wall Street ladder only to realize he was feeling depressed and unhealthy. He made a massive change by leaving his job to start Oura.

We became fast friends and saw right away that our business philosophies aligned. We struck a deal whereby I would invest in his company (which was valued at around $20 million at the time), and then it would hire our company to help it grow and scale. It was the perfect marriage to mint the new CTR.com ecosystem.

When it came time to sign the agreement, I realized that up until that moment—a moment that would forever make me believe in magic—I had overlooked one detail. It had nothing to do with numbers or percentages; neither was it anything the attorneys had brought to my attention.

It was Harpreet's last name. Because of our familiarity, I always called him Harpreet. But as my eyes focused on the DocuSign agreement on the screen in front of me, I started shaking.

Rai.

Harpreet Rai.

A memory came back to me, and I had goosebumps from head to toe. I closed my eyes for a moment and returned to the beachside store in Spain with the angelic woman who seemed to be communicating with me. "Never forget where you came from, trust the universe, and follow your heart."

The name of her store, if you recall, was Rai.

If that wasn't enough alchemy, in a few short years, we helped Harpreet Rai and his team from Oura grow to more than a $2.5 billion-dollar company that has positively impacted more than a million lives.

Together, we are living an expanded, conscious existence while playing the New Millionaire's game.

How you process this story, of course, is up to you. For me, I've stopped trying to understand the world logically. As a result, these incredible experiences have become the norm. I can't tell you how many times I say, "You can't make this shit up!"

Another way my perception has changed is my view of religion. Religion, much like every other institution, has become dogmatic, politicized, polarizing, and weaponized. It has more and more become a way to divide us instead of connect us. It's no wonder that so many of us have turned away from organized religion; however, it is paramount to realize that we may be throwing out the baby with the bathwater.

Even if I disagree with some of the teachings and much of the dogma of organized religion, there is wisdom from traditions, particularly your own. It does not matter whether you come from Christianity, Islam, Judaism, Hinduism, Buddhism, Sikhism, Taoism, or any other ancient wisdom tradition. There are consistent wisdom bombs that you will find across all of them that are relevant here and now and warrant some exploration and integration.

Whether or not you choose to explore the wisdom traditions you may come from, continue expanding your consciousness. When your consciousness expands, you become more open to the magic of synchronicities. Whatever the modality, by opening your heart, you'll start to see omens appearing in your life. They will help provide clues from the universe and confirmation that you're on the right path, creating ease and flow and inviting in more gratitude and inspiration.

By opening your heart, you'll start to see omens appearing in your life.

STILL NOT A BELIEVER? TRY SCIENCE

One of the biggest barriers to experiencing magic that society has created has been the politicization of science. Science is our best attempt to observe and explain the universe. It is *always* a work in progress and evolving. For example, Indians have been talking about the benefits of yoga and meditation for thousands of years, but science has only started validating these findings in the last few decades.

If something doesn't fit within the mainstream scientific explanation today, it gets labeled as pseudoscience and dismissed. "Follow the science" is what the mainstream says when something doesn't yet make complete sense to the human mind. Whenever someone says to look at the science, I always ask, "Who's funding this research?" What are the incentives of those who are funding specific scientific research studies? When you're "following the $cience," pay attention to how money influences the questions asked.

While I despise how science is used as a political pawn, ironically, it was science that convinced me that magic is real. Specifically, I'm talking about the placebo effect, which is a phenomenon in which some people experience a benefit in their physical health after receiving an inactive look-alike substance or treatment. This substance, or placebo, has no known medical effect and can be in the form of a pill (sugar pill), injection (saline solution), or other consumable.

Henry Beecher discovered the placebo effect as a medic in World War II. After running out of pain-killing morphine, he replaced it with a simple saline solution while continuing to tell the wounded soldiers it was morphine. It was a last-ditch effort to try to calm them, and to Beecher's surprise, it worked. By simply believing they were getting morphine, the soldiers felt better, and the placebo effect was born.

Placebo treatments have shown an ability to induce real responses in the brain. A patient's belief that treatment will work can release neurotransmitters, promote hormone production, ease pain, and boost overall mental and emotional wellness.[1] Big Pharma sees this as a nuisance and a threat to profits, because it knows that if everyone was aware of their healing abilities through the power of thought, it would not profit as much from selling expensive drugs. In fairness to Big Pharma, there's no real upside to talking about the power of magic.

The placebo effect is the magic of consciousness at work. If simply *believing* a treatment will work really can make us feel better, how much magic can we bring into our lives through the power of our thoughts?

THE FORMULA AND MEDITATION FOR MAGIC

I promised earlier that all it takes is seven minutes each day, and you will shift into a new reality.

I am going to share with you my life-changing MAGIC process and explain exactly how each of its five elements work. Here's how this will work: read the text below to understand the practice, the purpose, and the intention of each step. Then I encourage you to go to newmillionaires playbook.com to listen to the audio recording of the meditation. While the meditation only takes seven minutes of your time, putting in the effort to understand the practice before you start will make all the difference.

The core of this practice is the seven-minute MAGIC meditation, which somatically takes you through each element. This is where the magic really happens. It's what brings all the Keys together, supporting you in becoming the New Millionaire every single day. You will be able to create exactly what you desire. Here's the basic framework.

Magnetize: Through the visualization of a web of light, activate every cell in your body for you to become the most powerful magnet and attract all the possibilities your soul desires. Become the magnet, vibrate, sense it, feel it.

Alchemize: Transmute all unneeded energies and emotions into positive ones, and allow yourself to feel nothing turn into something.

Generate: Use heart energy to generate the vibrations and frequencies that will go back out through the web once your desire has been magnetized (brought in) and then alchemized (transmuted).

Inspire: Breathe into the universe the truth of what lights you up. Regain your own power and not just know, but also *feel*, that you control your own reality.

Clear: Bring your vision into reality through aligned action and surrender and enter the field of *nothingness*, where you are fully immersed in the present moment and existence beyond matter. This is the portal to magic.

Through practicing this meditation, you will activate and open the portals to magic.

1. Magnetize: Harness your thoughts to create your desired reality.

It's important to grasp our ability as human beings to attract people, places, and situations into our lives. It's kind of like how gravitational forces work in the solar system. When something moves closer or farther away, energy changes come into play. Similarly, we have the power to attract things into our lives based on our thoughts.

The first part of this step is to focus on connecting with a part of ourselves that emits an electromagnetic frequency. Our heart, for instance, has a strong magnetic field that extends out almost a meter.[2] When we generate positive thoughts and emotions and imagine our desired situation as if it has already happened, we activate this ability to attract what we want. Understanding this magnet-like ability is key and necessary before activation.

Take a moment to observe how you have the ability to connect with the infinite web that exists within you and extends out into the universe. Once you're plugged in, every cell in your body vibrates with magnetic energy, and you're now in a position to attract all the things that you desire.

2. Alchemize: Transform the nature of reality.

When we open ourselves up to new possibilities, our unconscious mind may also bring in thoughts and feelings that could hold us back, such as limiting beliefs and feelings of lack. These lower-frequency emotions can interfere with our true desires and influence what we attract into our lives. To align our energy with what we want, it's important to transmute these lower-frequency emotions into higher-frequency ones that support ourselves.

Limiting beliefs and fear are associated with low vibrational states, which can have a negative impact when projected back out into the universe. It's important to note that our limiting beliefs and feelings of lack are not just in our minds but are also stored in our bodies. In this step, we can shift the ways in which our body stores these limiting beliefs and emotions. This transmutation process involves the solar plexus, which is associated with confidence. By grounding ourselves and activating our solar plexus, we can alchemize our energy and feel the outcome in our bodies.

Take a moment to direct your breath toward your solar plexus, making sure to pay attention to the changes occurring in your body.

As we focus on the solar plexus, we may notice the energy transform within us. It's crucial to alchemize our energy before projecting it back out into the universe, to ensure that it aligns with our soul's true desires, free from any negative influences or sabotaging thoughts.

3. Generate: Cultivate elevated emotions that connect you with your desires.

Now it's time to cultivate the emotions that carry higher frequencies so we can connect with our desires. Be in the feelings that create the energetic vibration in the quantum field and draw that reality to you. When we are in a state of gratitude, we are receptive and connected to the universe.

Bring to mind all the things in your life that you are grateful for. It could be something as simple as a warm cup of tea, a kind smile from a stranger, or a roof over your head. As you focus on each thing, feel a sense of gratitude and appreciation for it. Allow these feelings to fill your heart and expand throughout your body.

When you embody the feeling that abundance is already yours, it truly becomes yours. You realize that abundance is not as simple or one-dimensional as "getting the mansion." Rather, it actually takes on an even greater form.

When you get into the state of already having, of feeling abundant, your brain sends out an electric signal. Using the elevated feeling state—as if it has already happened—your heart creates a magnetic field attracting this into your reality. When you are not in lack of something, it materializes.

Repeat this affirmation to yourself: "I am grateful for all the blessings in my life, big and small. I attract more abundance into my life every day." Cultivating a spirit of gratitude and abundance will attract more positive experiences and opportunities into your life. As you feel this healing elixir fill your body, the power of gratitude becomes you.

The other part of generating is giving to others. There are so many benefits of giving back, both obvious and subtle. It's in our nature to selflessly give to others; it's only society that has made us believe otherwise. The traditional economic model has led us to believe that we must compete for resources or end up with nothing.

The shift we are experiencing today takes us back to our roots—shifting from competition to collaboration in a community-centered model. Living in a world of competition is the same as living in a world of lack. But through sharing and leveraging resources, time, and skills, we strengthen the world around us and create a more abundant society. Simply put, when we "share the love," we generate more into our lives as well as for the larger whole.

4. Inspire: Breathe into the truth of what lights you up.

Inspire comes from the Latin *inspirare*, meaning "to breathe or blow into." The word was originally used to describe a divine or supernatural being imparting a truth or idea to someone. Breathe into the truth of what lights you up. Regain your own power and not just know, but also *feel*, that you control our own reality. Reach a state in which life happens through you.

Meditation, prayer, yoga, tai chi, and qigong are all practices that can support this process. One of the most powerful tools we can use is absolutely free and accessible at all times: breathwork.

Breathwork is the purest portal to the divine. Rather than feeling controlled by external forces (life happening *to* us), we are empowered to experience life happening *as* us.

Experience a fresh influx of energy, and expand your awareness around yourself, the world, and your purpose in life. Embrace your vulnerability and heightened sensitivity. Allow your breath to be a portal for life.

5. Clear: Bring your vision into reality through aligned action and surrender.

Bring your vision into reality through aligned action, release, and surrender, and embrace a sense of awe and wonder. *Allow*, but don't force. Consciousness is simply your *experience right now*, where all realities exist in the present moment. Consciousness constantly contracts and expands. When it contracts, you shut down and experience a smaller and more fearful reality. You live a mundane life of working, consuming, and numbing. Contraction blocks out magic.

Magic occurs when consciousness expands.

This is about letting go, surrendering. Lack and expectations carry weight, and the weight they add to your psychic load makes it feel as if the lack is real and makes you believe that you don't have access to what's available. Your expectation that something will happen—exactly the way you want it to happen—means that you are embodying and occupying the frequency of lack. This weight keeps you from the void of pure potentiality. In other words, when we hold on to every person and event that has wronged us, we allow the space and energy in our minds to be taken up with heaviness—space that could be filled with love and purpose, and energy that could be put into deepening consciousness and feeling more magic.

The real magic is to clear what blocks magic and naturally fall back into a state of nothingness.

When we get out of our own way, we experience an entire world of possibility. We see ourselves beyond the ego and get into the heart of who we are.

Visit newmillionairesplaybook.com to listen to the MAGIC meditation.

AFTER THE MAGIC MEDITATION

You have just tuned in to your heart's desire. Now it's time to take aligned action without attachment to an outcome. It could mean identifying one step you can take today that will move you closer to your goals. It could be as simple as making a phone call, forgiving a friend, letting go of a toxic relationship, or signing up for a course. Whatever it is, commit to taking action—or not. This is where you *allow* what wants to come through.

Regardless of what you actually do next, repeat this affirmation to yourself: "I am taking aligned action to create the life I desire. Every step I take brings me closer to my goals."

The seven-minute MAGIC meditation is one of the most powerfully effective hacks I use to create magic, and now it's yours. It gives you the perfect opportunity to tune in to what resonates with you in the moment and guides you to the pathway that you are meant to follow. Know that you have the power to create the life you desire.

HOW TO OPTIMIZE MAGIC: THE PINEAL GLAND, THE BEST KEPT SECRET

Now that you know how to create magic, I'm going to introduce you to a technique for supercharging it.

The pineal gland is so powerful, it can elicit a psychedelic experience such as the one I had sitting with the God molecule (But by no means am I specifically endorsing psychedelics or encouraging you to use them).

Psychedelics are a very personal experience. I am thrilled to see all the research occurring in this field, in part thanks to Tim Ferriss bringing both his platform and dollars to Johns Hopkins to study psychedelic drugs for addressing mental disorders as well as all the work Rick Doblin at the Multidisciplinary Association for Psychedelic Studies (MAPS) has done over the years to bring MDMA-assisted therapy into the mainstream. At the same time, I have concerns about psychedelics being used without the proper intention, support, and environment. As New Millionaires, you have the discernment to make an informed choice. I invite you to check out *How to Change Your Mind*, by Michael Pollan (also a series on Netflix) and

The Psychedelic Explorer's Guide: Safe, Therapeutic, and Sacred Journeys, by James Fadiman.

Another reason I've become less enthusiastic about psychedelics is that I've discovered how to create the same experience naturally. In part from studying with Dr. Joe Dispenza, I've learned how to create the psychedelic state by activating the pineal gland. This is the best kept secret of our anatomy and one that creates amazing opportunities for alchemy.

The pineal gland is a tiny, pine-cone-shaped gland deep in the center of your brain. As part of your endocrine system, it secretes the hormone melatonin and is important for sleep and regulating your circadian rhythm. In spiritual traditions, it's also known as the "third eye" due to its connection to our intuition. When activated through a fairly simple breathing technique, it can mimic the action of psychedelics (go to newmillionairesplaybook.com for this practice).

Think of the pineal gland as a transducer, like an antenna that converts the frequency of the quantum field into profound imagery. It is a liquid-crystal superconductor that sends as well as receives information through the transduction of energetic vibrational signals. When input coming through the pineal gland is processed, oxytocin is released, and other hormones are secreted through the pituitary gland. N-dimethyltryptamine (DMT), a hallucinogenic compound found in many plant and animal species, is also released here. This chemistry of cohesion, as well as pituitary and other gland signals, is sent out to your cells. The process allows your brain to tune in to higher-dimensional imagery and visuals that connect you with the universe.

Unfortunately, as with many things in current society, we are not set up to support our pineal gland. Instead, many aspects of our culture actually help calcify the pineal gland, affecting our ability to reach states of enlightenment and increasing our risk of neuronal diseases. Harmful chemicals are an intentional way for the Matrix to keep you from activating the pineal gland and experiencing natural, godlike states.

The pineal gland is glorious, and contrary to what you may have been told, you can access mind-blowing states of consciousness without any exogenous substances. When you experience your own power through activating the pineal gland, you will see yourself in that space of "nothingness" where anything is possible.

ONCE YOU SEE IT AND FEEL IT, YOU CAN ALWAYS BRING IT BACK

In our world of constant technological advancements, we often forget about technologies that were around long before the current day—technologies based on spirituality, which is *a connection to the human spirit or soul as opposed to material or physical things*. There are ancient traditional technologies that can help foster a deeper spiritual connection, allowing you to attain spiritual freedom, purpose, and abundance.

The most important thing to remember is that you have the full pharmacy inside of you. It's worth repeating: *consciousness is an inside job*. I've spent a lot of time, energy, and money looking for ways to hack consciousness. And while some of my adventures and esoteric discoveries were interesting, none were necessary. In fact, the more you think you need to *go somewhere* to discover magic, the less attainable it becomes. You don't need a guru, a silent retreat, or a psychedelic experience to bring magic into your life. It's more a process of letting go and opening up your heart.

Consciousness is an inside job.

If you believe in magic, it can serve as an inception point for you to open your portals and believe there is more than the three-dimensional world. If, even for a moment, you can see outside your existing reality, it will create new possibilities—and lead you to a place where you believe in infinite possibilities.

CHAPTER 7 POWER PLAY

❏ Practice the MAGIC meditation every day this week. Go to newmillionairesplaybook.com to listen to it.

CONCLUSION

YOU ARE
THE NEW
MILLIONAIRE

If success or failure of this planet and of human beings depended on how I am and what I do . . . How would I be? What would I do?

— **BUCKMINSTER FULLER**

Think about who you were before you began this journey. What have you learned? What has shifted? Who are you excited to become? Whatever vision you hold for yourself is entirely possible. When we get out of our own way, we experience an entire world of possibility. We see ourselves beyond the ego and get into the heart of who we are. Now it's about expanding to play with and experience the edges of your own existence.

We have gone on a journey that *starts with nothing and ends with everything.* It was by design that I started this chapter with a quote from Buckminster Fuller. He coined the term *ephemeralization*—the idea that technological advancement would one day allow humans to do "more and more with less and less until eventually you can do everything with nothing."[1]

When I read that, I don't see a bunch of robots vacuuming floors and tending to household chores. I see something much deeper. I see a world of flow and effortlessness. I see us operating outside the constraints of time and space and living an extraordinary existence.

I wrote this book because I believe that you, too, can conspire with the universe to make your dreams a reality. You can achieve the same outcomes with far less time, money, and heartache than it took me.

There's work to do to bring us back to a place of homeostasis. In fact, many of the opportunities we have now are a result of so many people being sick, angry, distracted, and scared. The forces pulling us back into a contracted state—whether you see them as profit-hungry tech companies or shadow organizations—are constantly arming themselves with more technology to control us.

The root cause of *all* of these problems is our **collective state of consciousness**. And until we address this, we will continue to create suffering for all living things on this planet.

The promising news is that our problems, including worsening mental health, create opportunities for new businesses. Harvard's Institute for Quantitative Social Science now has a Human Flourishing Program, which has developed a measurement-based approach to human flourishing based around five central domains: happiness and life-satisfaction; mental and physical health; meaning and purpose; character and virtue; and close social relationship. Wearable technology companies are making it easier to take control of our own health data to make decisions. At-home testing gives us access to the inner workings of our bodies. And the quantified self movement is pushing us to evolve into our highest state of consciousness.

As someone who invests in conscious businesses, I've seen where money has been going—and where it keeps heading. I'm also thrilled to say that most of the pitches I hear come from young entrepreneurs who care about humanity. If you're conscious, opportunities abound. Find a way to increase consciousness, and people will be lining up to fund your dream.

OMNI-WINS WILL SOON BE YOURS

Our goal is to be both heart-centered and pragmatic. Heart-opening experiences are part of our reality, as is returning to the "laundry" with a new perspective. We still put food on the table and meet our human needs while living a spiritual existence. For me, connecting to my heart is what allows me to create systems that lead to omni-wins.

Omni-wins, a term invented by Daniel Schmachtenberger, the co-founder of Neurohacker Collective and the Consilience Project, means creating abundance dynamics to have alignment with the well-being of others, ourselves, and society at large. What I like about Schmachtenberger is that he's both practical and philosophical. He said that to create omni-wins, "Disinformation is always disadvantageous to all involved, and transparency is optimally incentivized."[2] He also said, "If technology gives us something like the power of gods we have to have something like the love and wisdom of gods to be able to rightly wield it. Otherwise the misapplication of that power self-terminates."[3]

Together, as New Millionaires, we have everything we need to scale toward the power of the gods.

THE NEW MILLIONAIRE'S REALITY

Together we uncovered an entire world of possibilities. You've taken a journey with the intention of discovering how you can live a life of freedom, purpose, and abundance. You likely have an idea of what your life will look like ahead. As you read through each statement below, notice which ones stir up something in your soul more than others. Highlight them, if you please. These are your guideposts.

- To live life on your own terms

- To occupy multiple perspectives at once and not be overly attached to any one of them

- To live, work, and play in a way that serves your highest self vs. working a nine-to-five job for someone you despise

- To not accept your reality as is but to know that you can create whatever reality you desire

- To feel deeply aligned to your own inner power and truth

- To be free to choose love over fear

- To have a clear purpose in life and to move toward that purpose without external' pressure from powers and influences that don't have your best interest in mind or at heart

- To unapologetically show up as yourself and experience a reality wherein you are the master of your universe

- To experience life where you are not a product of your environment but rather, your environment is a product of you

- To allow your soul to traverse the multidimensionality of existence and experience realms and possibilities that would not otherwise be accessible

THE POWER OF COMPOUNDING CONSCIOUSNESS

It's part of my mission to positively impact one million lives through this book. Every reader creates a ripple effect. If this book (or any of our efforts) impacts a thousand lives, and that thousand impacts another thousand, a million lives will be impacted. Every step you take to advance consciousness brings you one step closer to becoming a New Millionaire.

I've used the same process that I used to hack the Internet to advance a Conscious Thought Revolution. When people ask that awkward question, "What do you do?" I tell them that I show people in all walks of life—from business associates and parents to scared teenagers and aspiring entrepreneurs—how to reclaim their own mind, body, and spirit to live a life of freedom and fulfillment.

When COVID-19 happened, I saw it as a test of our freedom, purpose, and abundance. It also tested our thoughts. It exposed some of my weaknesses, and thankfully, it also highlighted my strengths. I had a lens through which to understand the big picture, which, as it usually does, meant to follow the money. I also had the resources in place, for at least a few months, to endure food shortages. Feeling stress because of supply-chain issues is a sign of lacking sovereignty.

Rather than be riddled with fear and contract my consciousness, I was able to be an observer. This alone gave me the perspective to play my own game. Sure, I had tough moments, but because I wasn't dependent on the "system" for my kids' education and supplies, I wasn't a victim to public policy. This is the same freedom I want you to experience. It's why I created this playbook and why I continue to explore consciousness.

At CTR.com, you will not find the term *click-through rate*. Instead, you will see that Conscious Thought Revolution is a human-potential platform that measurably accelerates the evolution of consciousness. Part of that work is investing in companies. To entrepreneurs, pitch meetings seem standard until I hit them with *the trillion-dollar question*:

> How will this contribute to the transfer of hundreds of trillions of dollars over the next 25 years to measurably expand human consciousness?

There's no right or wrong answer. If there isn't any answer from the entrepreneurs—no matter how promising the financials look—I'm not interested. If there is, I put my heart and skills on the line to help companies to expand their profits while making an impact on human consciousness. These companies offer products like Oura (a ring that tracks sleep and health metrics), TRIPP (a digital wellness platform that unlocks awe, wonder, calm, and focus), *Endel* (an AI app for personalized soundscapes to help you focus, relax, and sleep), and Muse (a smart headband that acts as a personal meditation coach).

It's questions like the trillion-dollar one that have led people to take back their lives. Yes, questions—not declarations or edicts. My approach to this book mirrors the way I live my life: *ask questions that artfully lead you to self-reflect, and find your own answers.*

Congratulations on completing *The New Millionaire's Playbook*! You are on the path to freedom, purpose, and abundance, and you have an entire community at CTR supporting you. Go to **newmillionairesplaybook.com** to get access to all the bonus content. If you have any questions, or simply want to share what you got out of this book, please feel free to reach out to us as at hello@ctr .com. If you share any posts in relation to this journey, tag us: @consciousthoughtrevolution!

I'm excited for you to create the life you desire. Together, we are creating a brand-new game. With every game comes a set of rules. As we uncovered throughout this journey, the rules that were set in place over the past hundreds of years no longer serve us. It's time to reset the game completely and create new rules that are in service of our highest selves.

This is an act of revolutionary creativity. It's an opportunity to step into the life we truly want to live and carve a new path forward. You now have the Keys to think your own thoughts, create magic, and return to your soul.

With love and gratitude,
Gordy

ACKNOWLEDGMENTS

First, I want to thank my editorial team at Hay House Publishing, Lisa Cheng, and Monica O'Connor. Thank you for seeing the vision of this mission and supporting me in bringing this book to life in the most authentic way. Thank you for your kindness, flexibility, grace, and wisdom every step of the way.

Thanks to Jaidree Braddix, who has been an advocate for this book since the very beginning. You brought your passion, wisdom, and honesty to every part of this process, and your help over the course of the project has been impactful beyond words.

To Greg Dinkin, thank you for taking this journey with me. We learned a lot about ourselves and one another through this process, and I feel immensely grateful for your support in getting this book from an idea to a living entity. Sara Stibitz, thank you for bringing your superpowers to the table at such a crucial point. Your trust in me—and yourself—has been incredibly moving, and the book is so much better for having your imprint on it.

To my beautiful, incredible wife and counterpart, Sukhi, I could not have done this without you. The endless hours of support, late nights, smoothies, and endless wisdom that you bring—I could not be more blessed to have you by my side. Thank you for being my inspiration and muse, always.

To my boys, Jaxon, Jovie, and Julian, who are too young to read this book now, but you have been and always will be my greatest teachers in this lifetime—thank you. It is the greatest gift watching you grow into exactly who you are, and I could not be more proud to be your dad.

To my parents, Tuhādā Dhanvaad.

To Ashley and Tammy, thank you for your support and love throughout this process. For the laughter, the listening, the honest advice and feedback. Your mark on this book is felt on every page, and it's been so much more fun having you on this journey with me.

To Aaron and Haafiz, thank you for over a decade of friendship and growth. We've climbed some incredible mountains together (literally and metaphorically) and I know our journey is only beginning. Thank you for always encouraging me to be my best self and loving me through all of the lessons.

To Andrew, Dave, Harpreet, Tim, Nichol, Murph, Shefali, Malcolm, Sachin, Kollan, Phil, and Joe, thank you for being such epic humans, friends, and true embodiments of the New Millionaire. I am blessed and honored to have your wisdom infused throughout this book.

ENDNOTES

CHAPTER 1

1. John Grohol, "What Is Mass Formation Psychosis? Is It Like Mass Hysteria or Mass Delusion?" *New England Psychologist*, January 4, 2022, https://www.nepsy.com/articles/leading-stories/what-is-mass-formation-psychosis-is-it-like-mass-hysteria-or-mass-delusion/.

2. ASMR University, "ASMR Research Project," November 8, 2014, https://asmruniversity.com/asmr-survey/.

3. Sarah Vanbuskirk. "What Is a Brain Orgasm?" Verywell Mind, accessed April 21, 2023, https://www.verywellmind.com/what-is-a-brain-orgasm-5092957.

4. Techopedia, "Reality Distortion Field," October 7, 2012, https://www.techopedia.com/definition/23694/reality-distortion-field-rdf.

5. Adam Webb, "Harnessing the Power of Your Reality Distortion Field," *Forbes*, accessed April 21, 2023, https://www.forbes.com/sites/forbesbusinessdevelopmentcouncil/2021/10/04/harnessing-the-power-of-your-reality-distortion-field/.

6. Ibid.

7. ChangingWinds, "Steve Jobs' Reality Distortion Field: Leadership or Bullying?," November 18, 2018, https://changingwinds.wordpress.com/2018/11/18/steve-jobs-reality-distortion-field-leadership-or-bullying/.

8. Firth, Joseph, John Torous, Brendon Stubbs, Josh A. Firth, Genevieve Z. Steiner, Lee Smith, Mario Alvarez-Jimenez, et al., "The 'Online Brain': How the Internet May Be Changing Our Cognition," *World Psychiatry* 18, no. 2 (June 2019): 119–29, https://doi.org/10.1002/wps.20617.

9. Michigan State University, "Excessive Social Media Use Is Comparable to Drug Addiction," *MSU* Today, accessed April 21, 2023, https://msutoday.msu.edu/news/2019/excessive-social-media-use-is-comparable-to-drug-addiction.

10. Piyush Sharma, "Elon Musk's Philosophical Take On Why He Is Does What He Does Is An Inspiration To All Of Us," MensXP, February 26, 2018, https://www.mensxp.com/work-life/entrepreneurship/42904-elon-musk-s-philosophical-take-on-why-he-is-does-what-he-does-is-an-inspiration-to-all-of-us.html.

CHAPTER 2

1. "Anxiety Disorders," NAMI: National Alliance on Mental Illness, accessed April 21, 2023, https://www.nami.org/About-Mental-Illness/Mental-Health-Conditions/Anxiety-Disorders.

2. Jim Clifton, "The World's Broken Workplace," Gallup.com, June 13, 2017, https://news.gallup.com/opinion/chairman/212045/world-broken-workplace.aspx.

3. Wilkes, Juliet, Gulcan Garip, Yasuhiro Kotera, and Dean Fido, "Can Ikigai Predict Anxiety, Depression, and Well-Being?" *International Journal of Mental Health and Addiction* (2022): 1–13, https://doi.org/10.1007/s11469-022-00764-7.

4. Suzy Batiz, "Alive as Shit," Suzy Batiz, accessed April 21, 2023, https://suzybatiz.com/.

5. Ibid.

CHAPTER 3

1. World Health Organization, Regional Office for South-East Asia, "Health Systems in Transition," *The Kingdom of Bhutan Health System Review,* Vol. 7, No. 2 (2017) https://apps.who.int/iris/handle/10665/255701.

2. Annie Kelly, "Gross National Happiness in Bhutan: The Big Idea from a Tiny State That Could Change the World," *The Guardian,* December 1, 2012, World news section, https://www.theguardian.com/world/2012/dec/01/bhutan-wealth-happiness-counts.

3. Matthieu Ricard, "UN High Level Meeting on Wellbeing and Happiness: Defining and New Economic Paradigm, Matthieu Ricard (blog), accessed April 21, 2023, https://www.matthieuricard.org/en/blog/posts/un-high-level-meeting-on-wellbeing-and-happiness-defining-and-new-economic-paradigm.

4. The Work of Byron Katie, "Do The Work," The Work, accessed April 21, 2023, https://thework.com/instruction-the-work-byron-katie/.

5. Ibid.

6. James Clear, "Make Your Life Better by Saying Thank You in These 7 Situations," James Clear, https://jamesclear.com/say-thank-you.

7. Harvard Health. "Heart Rate Variability: How It Might Indicate Well-Being," November 22, 2017. https://www.health.harvard.edu/blog/heart-rate-variability-new-way-track-well-2017112212789.

8. Stephen D. Edwards, David J. Edwards, Richard Honeycutt, "Heart-Math as an Integrative, Personal, Social, and Global Healthcare System," *Healthcare* 10, no. 2 (2022), https://doi.org/10.3390/healthcare10020376.

9. Ibid.

10. Ibid.

CHAPTER 4

1. Michael Seidlinger, "Rich Dad, Poor Dad: 25 Years of Financial Advice Books," PublishersWeekly.com, accessed April 21, 2023, https://www.publishersweekly.com/pw/by-topic/industry-news/people/article/89314-rich-dad-poor-dad-25-years-of-financial-advice-books.html.

2. Simon & Schuster, "Robert T. Kiyosaki," Authors, accessed April 21, 2023, https://www.simonandschuster.com/authors/Robert-T-Kiyosaki/42817948.

3. Ray Kurzweil, "10 Questions for Ray Kurzweil," *TIME,* accessed April 21, 2023, https://content.time.com/time/magazine/article/0,9171,2033076,00.html.

4. Fuller Buckminster, *Operating Manual for Spaceship Earth* (New York: E.P. Dutton & Co., 1969), 1.4.

5. Mike Kresse, "Will We See the End of Cash by 2030?" FIS Global, accessed April 21, 2023, https://www.fisglobal.com/zh-cn/fintech2030/connectivity/cashless-society-2030.

6. Strategic Market Research, LLP, "Metaverse in Gaming Market – Insights on $663.8 Billion Industry Opportunity, The Next Frontier or Hype?" GlobeNewswire, December 28, 2022, https://www.globenewswire.com/en/news-release/2022/12/28/2580214/0/en/Metaverse-in-Gaming-Market-Insights-on-663-8-Billion-Industry-Opportunity-The-Next-Frontier-or-Hype.html.

7. Bernard Marr, "How To Buy Land & Real Estate In The Metaverse," *Forbes,* accessed April 19, 2023, https://www.forbes.com/sites/bernardmarr/2022/03/23/how-to-buy-land--real-estate-in-the-metaverse/.

8. Christine Moy and Adit Gadgil, "Opportunities in the metaverse: How businesses can explore the metaverse and navigate the hype vs. reality," J.P. Morgan, 2022, https://www.jpmorgan.com/content/dam/jpm/treasury-services/documents/opportunities-in-the-metaverse.pdf.

CHAPTER 5

1. Remy Blumenfeld, "How a 15,000-Year-Old Human Bone Could Help You Through the Coronacrisis," *Forbes*, accessed April 24, 2023, https://www.forbes.com/sites/remyblumenfeld/2020/03/21/how-a-15000-year-old-human-bone-could-help-you-through-the--coronavirus/.

2. Robert Winston and Rebecca Chicot, "The Importance of Early Bonding on the Long-Term Mental Health and Resilience of Children," *London Journal of Primary Care* 8, no. 1 (February 24, 2016): 12–14, https://doi.org/10.1080/17571472.2015.1133012.

3. Nicholas A. Christakis and James H. Fowler, "The Collective Dynamics of Smoking in a Large Social Network," *New England Journal of Medicine* 358, no. 21 (May 22, 2008): 2249–58, https://doi.org/10.1056/NEJMsa0706154.

4. Jiddu Krishnamurti, *On Relationship* (Harper Collins, 1992).

CHAPTER 6

1. Carol Wiebe, "Here Is a Great Quote by Einstein about the Wave-Particle Duality: 'It Seems as Though We Must Use…,'" *Medium* (blog), April 25, 2016, https://medium.com/@carolwiebe/here-is-a-great-quote-by-einstein-about-the-wave-particle-duality-it-seems-as-though-we-must-use-118140925f3b.

2. "Maslow's Hierarchy of Needs Is Incomplete—There's a Final, Forgotten Stage," *Big Think* (blog), accessed April 24, 2023, https://bigthink.com/videos/nichol-bradford-on-self-transcendence-and-maslows-hierarchy/.

3. "Warrior Definition—Google Search," accessed April 24, 2023, https://www.google.com/search?q=Warrior+Definition&client=firefox-b-1-d&biw=1208&bih=2639&sxsrf=APwXEdfRRz0uEpsLReWdZi0LpOGcSuevwg%3A1682350785969&ei=waJGZKraOrWuqtsP5fWqqAw&ved=0ahUKEwjqvvCH7cL-AhU1l2oFHeW6CsUQ4dUDCA8&uact=5&oq=Warrior+Definition&gs_lcp=Cgxnd3Mtd2l6LXNlcnAQAzIJCCMQJxBGEPkBMgUIABCABADIKCAAQgAQQFBCHAjIFCAAQgAQyBQgAEIAEMggUIABCABDIFCAAQgAQyBQgAEIAEMggIABCKBRCGAzIICAAQigUQhgM6BAgAEEc6BAgjECc6CgguEIoFENQCEM6BwgAEIFEEM6DQgAEIoFELEDEIMBEEM6DQguEIoFELEDEIMBEEM6CAgAEIoFEJECCgoILhCABBAUEIcCSgQIQRRgAUMMEWN8WYOQWaABwAngCgAHiAYgBjAeSAQU1LjIuMZgBAKABAcgBCMMABAQ&sclient=gws-wiz-serp.

4. Alex Hoegler, "Top 15 Greatest NHL Rivalries of All Time," TheSportster, November 17, 2015, https://www.thesportster.com/hockey/top-15-greatest-nhl-rivalries-of-all-time/.

5. CBC News, "Riots Erupt in Vancouver after Canucks Loss," CBC, June 16, 2011, https://www.cbc.ca/news/canada/british-columbia/riots-erupt-in-vancouver-after-canucks-loss-1.993707.

6. The Canadian Press, "Nine Cops Hurt, 150 Injured during Vancouver Riot," CP24, June 16, 2011, https://www.cp24.com/nine-cops-hurt-150-injured-during-vancouver-riot-1.657648.

CHAPTER 7

1. Harvard Health, "The Power of the Placebo Effect," Harvard Health Publishing, December 13, 2021, https://www.health.harvard.edu/mental-health/the-power-of-the-placebo-effect.

2. HeartMath Institute, "Chapter 06: Energetic Communication," accessed April 25, 2023, https://www.heartmath.org/research/science-of-the-heart/energetic-communication/.

CONCLUSION

1. R. Buckminster Fuller, *Nine Chains to the Moon* (Estate of R. Buckminster Fuller, 2000).

2. "New Economics Series: Part 2," *Daniel Schmachtenberger* (blog), October 12, 2017, https://civilizationemerging.com/new-economics-series-2/.

3. Daniel Schmachtenberger says [@DanielSchmacht1], "'If Technology Gives Us Something like the Power of Gods We Have to Have Something like the Love and Wisdom of Gods to Be Able to Rightly Wield It. Otherwise the Misapplication of That Power Self-Terminates.' Https://T.Co/3sdMmLjlrT," Tweet, *Twitter*, July 26, 2020, https://twitter.com/DanielSchmacht1/status/1287383254455255040.

ABOUT THE AUTHOR

 **Gordy Bal** is a heart-centered entrepreneur, impact investor, and visionary leader who helps people generate true abundance by stepping into their purpose to make a meaningful impact. With his unwavering commitment to catalyzing positive transformation, Gordy founded the influential Conscious Thought Revolution (CTR), a vibrant community of change-makers who are passionate about utilizing their talents and resources to make a difference.

At CTR, Gordy's aim is to accelerate the evolution of human consciousness and create a future where humanity and the planet can thrive harmoniously. Gordy Bal's approach is grounded in the belief that by tapping into our deepest potential and aligning our actions with our inner truth, we can unlock extraordinary possibilities for ourselves and the world around us. Harnessing this commitment, Gordy has dedicated himself to creating a world where business, finance, and human consciousness seamlessly co-exist.

With over a decade of trailblazing experience in digital marketing, Gordy's expertise has been instrumental in cultivating industry-leading companies. As the pioneering force behind the Conscious Capital Venture Fund, Gordy has spearheaded the transformation of early startups into billion-dollar powerhouses. Gordy has become a highly sought after advisor, mentor and coach to entrepreneurs and investors seeking his unparalleled guidance.

Gordy's passionate pursuits extend far beyond financial realms, delving into the intersection of science, technology, and spirituality. Holding a degree in Psychology with a neuroscience emphasis, he remains at the vanguard of cutting-edge research in these fields, forging an inspiring body of work centered around the profound notion that thoughts are the ultimate form of currency.

Beyond his exceptional achievements, Gordy cherishes the roles of devoted husband and loving father to three spirited boys. Gordy Bal continues to redefine the boundaries of possibility, inspiring millions of individuals to join him on the path to a brighter future.

ctr.com

Hay House Titles of Related Interest

All of the above are available at your local bookstore,
or may be ordered by contacting Hay House (see next page).

***

We hope you enjoyed this Hay House book. If you'd like to receive our online catalog featuring additional information on Hay House books and products, or if you'd like to find out more about the Hay Foundation, please contact:

Hay House, Inc., P.O. Box 5100, Carlsbad, CA 92018-5100
(760) 431-7695 or (800) 654-5126
(760) 431-6948 (fax) or (800) 650-5115 (fax)
www.hayhouse.com® • www.hayfoundation.org

———

Published in Australia by: Hay House Australia Pty. Ltd.,
18/36 Ralph St., Alexandria NSW 2015
Phone: 612-9669-4299 • *Fax:* 612-9669-4144
www.hayhouse.com.au

Published in the United Kingdom by: Hay House UK, Ltd.,
The Sixth Floor, Watson House, 54 Baker Street, London W1U 7BU
Phone: +44 (0)20 3927 7290 • *Fax:* +44 (0)20 3927 7291
www.hayhouse.co.uk

Published in India by: Hay House Publishers India,
Muskaan Complex, Plot No. 3, B-2, Vasant Kunj, New Delhi 110 070
Phone: 91-11-4176-1620 • *Fax:* 91-11-4176-1630
www.hayhouse.co.in

———

Access New Knowledge.
Anytime. Anywhere.

Learn and evolve at your own pace
with the world's leading experts.

www.hayhouseU.com